3/94

The Department of Defense

KNOW YOUR GOVERNMENT

The Department of Defense

Andrew Cohen
and
Beth Heinsohn

CHELSEA HOUSE PUBLISHERS

On the cover: An aerial view of the Pentagon, headquarters of the Department of Defense, located in Arlington, Virginia.
Frontispiece: A gunnery sergeant from a Marine Corps helicopter squadron mans a .50-caliber machine gun while on a 1987 mission in the Persian Gulf.

Chelsea House Publishers
Editor-in-Chief: Nancy Toff
Executive Editor: Remmel T. Nunn
Managing Editor: Karyn Gullen Browne
Copy Chief: Juliann Barbato
Picture Editor: Adrian G. Allen
Art Director: Maria Epes
Manufacturing Manager: Gerald Levine

Know Your Government
Senior Editor: Kathy Kuhtz

Staff for THE DEPARTMENT OF DEFENSE
Assistant Editor: Karen Schimmel
Copy Editor: Michael Goodman
Deputy Copy Chief: Nicole Bowen
Editorial Assistant: Gregory R. Rodríguez
Picture Researcher: Bill Rice
Picture Coordinator: Melanie Sanford
Assistant Art Director: Loraine Machlin
Senior Designer: Noreen M. Lamb
Production Manager: Joseph Romano
Production Coordinator: Marie Claire Cebrián

3 5 7 9 8 6 4 2

Library of Congress Cataloging-in-Publication Data
Cohen, Andy.
  The Department of Defense/Andy Cohen and Beth Heinsohn.
    p.   cm.—(Know your government)
  Includes bibliographical references.
  Summary: Surveys the history of the Department of Defense and
describes its structure, current function, and influence on American society.
  ISBN 0-87754-837-4
      0-7910-0886-X (pbk.)
  1. United States. Dept. of Defense—Juvenile literature.
  [1. United States. Dept. of Defense.] I. Heinsohn, Beth.
  II. Title.   III. Series: Know your government series.
                                                                89-22297
UA23.6.C64   1990   CIP
353.6—dc20   AC

CONTENTS

KNOW YOUR GOVERNMENT

CHELSEA HOUSE PUBLISHERS

INTRODUCTION

Government: Crises of Confidence

Arthur M. Schlesinger, jr.

From the start, Americans have regarded their government with a mixture of reliance and mistrust. The men who founded the republic did not doubt the indispensability of government. "If men were angels," observed the 51st Federalist Paper, "no government would be necessary." But men are not angels. Because human beings are subject to wicked as well as to noble impulses, government was deemed essential to assure freedom and order.

At the same time, the American revolutionaries knew that government could also become a source of injury and oppression. The men who gathered in Philadelphia in 1787 to write the Constitution therefore had two purposes in mind. They wanted to establish a strong central authority and to limit that central authority's capacity to abuse its power.

To prevent the abuse of power, the Founding Fathers wrote two basic principles into the new Constitution. The principle of federalism divided power between the state governments and the central authority. The principle of the separation of powers subdivided the central authority itself into three branches—the executive, the legislative, and the judiciary—so that "each may be a check on the other." The *Know Your Government* series focuses on the major executive departments and agencies in these branches of the federal government.

The Constitution did not plan the executive branch in any detail. After vesting the executive power in the president, it assumed the existence of "executive departments" without specifying what these departments should be. Congress began defining their functions in 1789 by creating the Departments of State, Treasury, and War. The secretaries in charge of these departments made up President Washington's first cabinet. Congress also provided for a legal officer, and President Washington soon invited the attorney general, as he was called, to attend cabinet meetings. As need required, Congress created more executive departments.

Setting up the cabinet was only the first step in organizing the American state. With almost no guidance from the Constitution, President Washington, seconded by Alexander Hamilton, his brilliant secretary of the treasury, equipped the infant republic with a working administrative structure. The Federalists believed in both executive energy and executive accountability and set high standards for public appointments. The Jeffersonian opposition had less faith in strong government and preferred local government to the central authority. But when Jefferson himself became president in 1801, although he set out to change the direction of policy, he found no reason to alter the framework the Federalists had erected.

By 1801 there were about 3,000 federal civilian employees in a nation of a little more than 5 million people. Growth in territory and population steadily enlarged national responsibilities. Thirty years later, when Jackson was president, there were more than 11,000 government workers in a nation of 13 million. The federal establishment was increasing at a faster rate than the population.

Jackson's presidency brought significant changes in the federal service. He believed that the executive branch contained too many officials who saw their jobs as "species of property" and as "a means of promoting individual interest." Against the idea of a permanent service based on life tenure, Jackson argued for the periodic redistribution of federal offices, contending that this was the democratic way and that official duties could be made "so plain and simple that men of intelligence may readily qualify themselves for their performance." He called this policy rotation-in-office. His opponents called it the spoils system.

In fact, partisan legend exaggerated the extent of Jackson's removals. More than 80 percent of federal officeholders retained their jobs. Jackson discharged no larger a proportion of government workers than Jefferson had done a generation earlier. But the rise in these years of mass political parties gave federal patronage new importance as a means of building the party and of rewarding activists. Jackson's successors were less restrained in the distribu-

8

tion of spoils. As the federal establishment grew—to nearly 40,000 by 1861—the politicization of the public service excited increasing concern.

After the Civil War the spoils system became a major political issue. High-minded men condemned it as the root of all political evil. The spoilsmen, said the British commentator James Bryce, "have distorted and depraved the mechanism of politics." Patronage, by giving jobs to unqualified, incompetent, and dishonest persons, lowered the standards of public service and nourished corrupt political machines. Office-seekers pursued presidents and cabinet secretaries without mercy. "Patronage," said Ulysses S. Grant after his presidency, "is the bane of the presidential office." "Every time I appoint someone to office," said another political leader, "I make a hundred enemies and one ingrate." George William Curtis, the president of the National Civil Service Reform League, summed up the indictment. He said,

> The theory which perverts public trusts into party spoils, making public
> employment dependent upon personal favor and not on proved merit,
> necessarily ruins the self-respect of public employees, destroys the
> function of party in a republic, prostitutes elections into a desperate
> strife for personal profit, and degrades the national character by lower-
> ing the moral tone and standard of the country.

The object of civil service reform was to promote efficiency and honesty in the public service and to bring about the ethical regeneration of public life. Over bitter opposition from politicians, the reformers in 1883 passed the Pendleton Act, establishing a bipartisan Civil Service Commission, competitive examinations, and appointment on merit. The Pendleton Act also gave the president authority to extend by executive order the number of "classified" jobs—that is, jobs subject to the merit system. The act applied initially only to about 14,000 of the more than 100,000 federal positions. But by the end of the 19th century 40 percent of federal jobs had moved into the classified category.

Civil service reform was in part a response to the growing complexity of American life. As society grew more organized and problems more technical, official duties were no longer so plain and simple that any person of intelligence could perform them. In public service, as in other areas, the all-round man was yielding ground to the expert, the amateur to the professional. The excesses of the spoils system thus provoked the counter-ideal of scientific public administration, separate from politics and, as far as possible, insulated against it.

The cult of the expert, however, had its own excesses. The idea that administration could be divorced from policy was an illusion. And in the realm of policy, the expert, however much segregated from partisan politics, can

9

never attain perfect objectivity. He remains the prisoner of his own set of values. It is these values rather than technical expertise that determine fundamental judgments of public policy. To turn over such judgments to experts, moreover, would be to abandon democracy itself; for in a democracy final decisions must be made by the people and their elected representatives. "The business of the expert," the British political scientist Harold Laski rightly said, "is to be on tap and not on top."

Politics, however, were deeply ingrained in American folkways. This meant intermittent tension between the presidential government, elected every four years by the people, and the permanent government, which saw presidents come and go while it went on forever. Sometimes the permanent government knew better than its political masters; sometimes it opposed or sabotaged valuable new initiatives. In the end a strong president with effective cabinet secretaries could make the permanent government responsive to presidential purpose, but it was often an exasperating struggle.

The struggle within the executive branch was less important, however, than the growing impatience with bureaucracy in society as a whole. The 20th century saw a considerable expansion of the federal establishment. The Great Depression and the New Deal led the national government to take on a variety of new responsibilities. The New Deal extended the federal regulatory apparatus. By 1940, in a nation of 130 million people, the number of federal workers for the first time passed the 1 million mark. The Second World War brought federal civilian employment to 3.8 million in 1945. With peace, the federal establishment declined to around 2 million by 1950. Then growth resumed, reaching 2.8 million by the 1980s.

The New Deal years saw rising criticism of "big government" and "bureaucracy." Businessmen resented federal regulation. Conservatives worried about the impact of paternalistic government on individual self-reliance, on community responsibility, and on economic and personal freedom. The nation in effect renewed the old debate between Hamilton and Jefferson in the early republic, although with an ironic exchange of positions. For the Hamiltonian constituency, the "rich and well-born," once the advocate of affirmative government, now condemned government intervention, while the Jeffersonian constituency, the plain people, once the advocate of a weak central government and of states' rights, now favored government intervention.

In the 1980s, with the presidency of Ronald Reagan, the debate has burst out with unusual intensity. According to conservatives, government intervention abridges liberty, stifles enterprise, and is inefficient, wasteful, and arbitrary. It disturbs the harmony of the self-adjusting market and creates worse troubles than it solves. Get government off our backs, according to the popular cliché, and our problems will solve themselves. When government is necessary, let it be at the local level, close to the people. Above all, stop the inexorable growth of the federal government.

In fact, for all the talk about the "swollen" and "bloated" bureaucracy, the federal establishment has not been growing as inexorably as many Americans seem to believe. In 1949, it consisted of 2.1 million people. Thirty years later, while the country had grown by 70 million, the federal force had grown only by 750,000. Federal workers were a smaller percentage of the population in 1985 than they were in 1955—or in 1940. The federal establishment, in short, has not kept pace with population growth. Moreover, national defense and the postal service account for 60 percent of federal employment.

Why then the widespread idea about the remorseless growth of government? It is partly because in the 1960s the national government assumed new and intrusive functions: affirmative action in civil rights, environmental protection, safety and health in the workplace, community organization, legal aid to the poor. Although this enlargement of the federal regulatory role was accompanied by marked growth in the size of government on all levels, the expansion has taken place primarily in state and local government. Whereas the federal force increased by only 27 percent in the 30 years after 1950, the state and local government force increased by an astonishing 212 percent.

Despite the statistics, the conviction flourishes in some minds that the national government is a steadily growing behemoth swallowing up the liberties of the people. The foes of Washington prefer local government, feeling it is closer to the people and therefore allegedly more responsive to popular needs. Obviously there is a great deal to be said for settling local questions locally. But local government is characteristically the government of the locally powerful. Historically, the way the locally powerless have won their human and constitutional rights has often been through appeal to the national government. The national government has vindicated racial justice against local bigotry, defended the Bill of Rights against local vigilantism, and protected natural resources against local greed. It has civilized industry and secured the rights of labor organizations. Had the states' rights creed prevailed, there would perhaps still be slavery in the United States.

The national authority, far from diminishing the individual, has given most Americans more personal dignity and liberty than ever before. The individual freedoms destroyed by the increase in national authority have been in the main the freedom to deny black Americans their rights as citizens; the freedom to put small children to work in mills and immigrants in sweatshops; the freedom to pay starvation wages, require barbarous working hours, and permit squalid working conditions; the freedom to deceive in the sale of goods and securities; the freedom to pollute the environment—all freedoms that, one supposes, a civilized nation can readily do without.

"Statements are made," said President John F. Kennedy in 1963, "labelling the Federal Government an outsider, an intruder, an adversary. . . . The United States Government is not a stranger or not an enemy. It is the people of fifty states joining in a national effort. . . . Only a great national effort by a great people working together can explore the mysteries of space, harvest the products at the bottom of the ocean, and mobilize the human, natural, and material resources of our lands."

So an old debate continues. However, Americans are of two minds. When pollsters ask large, spacious questions—Do you think government has become too involved in your lives? Do you think government should stop regulating business?—a sizable majority opposes big government. But when asked specific questions about the practical work of government—Do you favor social security? unemployment compensation? Medicare? health and safety standards in factories? environmental protection? government guarantee of jobs for everyone seeking employment? price and wage controls when inflation threatens?—a sizable majority approves of intervention.

In general, Americans do not want less government. What they want is more efficient government. They want government to do a better job. For a time in the 1970s, with Vietnam and Watergate, Americans lost confidence in the national government. In 1964, more than three-quarters of those polled had thought the national government could be trusted to do right most of the time. By 1980 only one-quarter was prepared to offer such trust. But by 1984 trust in the federal government to manage national affairs had climbed back to 45 percent.

Bureaucracy is a term of abuse. But it is impossible to run any large organization, whether public or private, without a bureaucracy's division of labor and hierarchy of authority. And we live in a world of large organizations. Without bureaucracy modern society would collapse. The problem is not to abolish bureaucracy, but to make it flexible, efficient, and capable of innovation.

Two hundred years after the drafting of the Constitution, Americans still regard government with a mixture of reliance and mistrust—a good combination. Mistrust is the best way to keep government reliable. Informed criticism

12

is the means of correcting governmental inefficiency, incompetence, and arbitrariness; that is, of best enabling government to play its essential role. For without government, we cannot attain the goals of the Founding Fathers. Without an understanding of government, we cannot have the informed criticism that makes government do the job right. It is the duty of every American citizen to know our government—which is what this series is all about.

In September 1982, U.S. Marines stationed in Beirut, Lebanon, await transportation that will return them to the United States. Approximately one-fourth of the 2 million active-duty military personnel employed by the Department of Defense serve outside the United States.

ONE

The Defense of
a Nation

The Department of Defense (DOD) is entrusted with protecting the safety and security of the United States. It employs more than 3 million people, both military and civilian, and spends nearly $300 billion per year. It is one of the most powerful and important institutions in American life and plays a significant role on the world scene as well. If the DOD were a private corporation rather than a government agency, it would have twice the operating capital of Exxon, America's largest corporation, and more than four times the number of people on its payroll than General Motors, the nation's largest employer.

The DOD has authority over all military matters in the United States, from marching boots to B-1 bombers, but it would be a mistake to regard it as strictly a military organization made up of the U.S. Army, Navy, Air Force, and Marine Corps. (A fourth service, the Coast Guard, is part of the Department of Transportation in peacetime but in times of war comes under the direction of the U.S. Navy.) Though it includes these elements, the DOD is also a political and administrative institution responsible for the many activities of modern defense—from the development of weapons and related technology to the use of troops in peacekeeping activities and the formation and management of defense policy. The secretary of defense does not fire a weapon or command troops, but he and his subordinates are responsible for issuing orders to those who do and for supervising all aspects of military planning.

The DOD is popularly known as the Pentagon, after the massive five-sided building in Arlington, Virginia (just across the Potomac River from Washington, D.C.), where the Defense Department is headquartered. When the Pentagon building was completed in 1943, it was the world's largest office building, covering 3.7 million square feet of usable floor space. But the Pentagon is a good deal more than just a big building. It has loomed large in the post–World War II era as a vivid and distinct symbol of America's formidable military might, political power, and influence on the world's stage. Whether in Moscow or London, Bogotá or Beijing, the name and image of the Pentagon is representative of everything that gives the United States superpower status.

The Mission of the DOD

The primary purpose of the U.S. military is to assure the security and survival of the United States as a free and independent nation. To this end, the American armed forces are concerned not only with protecting the borders and coastlines of the United States but also with defending the country's vital interests. These interests are usually defined as the right and ability of the citizens of the United States and its allies to conduct business, travel, express thoughts and ideas, and live freely at home and abroad.

This commitment to protecting national security and freedom includes America's post–World War II pledge to defend the territory of its many allies all over the world in order to preserve the ideals and integrity of Western democracy and capitalism. One of the first manifestations of this pledge was the creation in 1949 of the North Atlantic Treaty Organization (NATO), by which the United States formally bound itself to its Western European allies, among them Great Britain, France, Italy, and Denmark. The idea behind NATO is collective security—the commitment of NATO's member nations to defend each other if any one of them is attacked by a hostile power. In 1949, the biggest fear—indeed, the only fear—of NATO members was an attack from the Soviet Union and its allies. To this day, nearly half of the United States's total military budget is spent on the defense of foreign allies, the first line of America's defenses.

The Nuclear Age

The first use of nuclear weapons in August 1945, when the United States dropped the atomic bomb on the Japanese cities of Hiroshima and Nagasaki to bring an end to World War II, demonstrated how weapons of mass destruction can be used as instruments of limited military goals. (Traditionally, the goal of war and its weapons was total destruction of the enemy's forces. In the case of Japan the use of the atomic bomb prompted the immediate surrender of Japanese forces and avoided an all-out invasion. President Truman's estimate of the number of American lives that would be lost in such an invasion was 1 million. At least as many Japanese soldiers and civilians would also have died. The Hiroshima and Nagasaki bombings claimed some 200,000 lives.) Almost a year later, in June 1946, Bernard Brodie, a professor of international politics at Yale University, wrote, "Thus far the chief purpose of our military establishment has been to win wars. From now on its chief purpose must be to avert them. It can have almost no other purpose." This concept, known as deterrence, remains the official U.S. policy guiding the use of nuclear weapons.

A great deal of expense goes into maintaining nuclear deterrence. The idea is that the United States and its allies can deter, or prevent, a Soviet nuclear attack by vowing to retaliate in kind. In the 1950s, this was known as the policy of massive retaliation, though by the early 1960s it came to be known as mutual assured destruction (also known by the acronym MAD). The basis for this policy is the belief that no sane national leader would initiate the use of nuclear weapons if he or she thought it would mean risking massive nuclear destruction

The remains of a building in Hiroshima, Japan, in September 1945—one month after the United States dropped the world's first atomic bomb on the city. The atomic bomb's potential for mass destruction gave rise to the concept of deterrence, whereby the United States hopes to prevent a nuclear attack by the Soviet Union by vowing to retaliate.

17

in return. Security lies in neither side wishing to pay such a high price for an initial surprise attack.

The problem for U.S. defense planners is to make sure that a first strike, or surprise attack, by the Soviet Union does not destroy the United States's ability to strike back. The answer to this problem is what is known as the strategic triad, the backbone of American nuclear defense policy. At any given moment, 24 hours a day, 365 days a year, thousands of uniformed U.S. Air Force and Navy personnel in bombers, submarines, and missile command centers all over the world are prepared to attack the Soviet Union with nuclear weapons should they receive the order from their commander in chief, the president of the United States. The idea behind the three "legs" of the triad (airborne, seaborne, and land based) is that it would be impossible for the Soviet Union to eliminate U.S. retaliatory power with a first strike, because some elements of the triad would survive.

Challenges for the DOD

The DOD is relatively young as government agencies go. It was officially created on July 26, 1947, with the passage of the National Security Act. (However, it was not called the Department of Defense until 1949.) Before 1947, the defense of the United States fell to the president, as commander in chief, the Department of War (established in 1789), and the Department of the Navy (established in 1798). The National Security Act of 1947 combined the War Department and the Navy Department, as well as the newly created Department of the Air Force, under a single organization, called the National Military Establishment, headed by a civilian secretary of defense.

By 1947, the defense of the United States had come to include both the management of the atomic bomb and a kind of alliance making that required the permanent stationing of U.S. troops abroad. The DOD reflects these modern developments in the worldwide scope of its mission; in its massive, highly differentiated structure; in the importance it assigns to nuclear arms control; in the changing nature of its place in American foreign policy; and in its large role as a buyer of U.S. goods and an employer of Americans.

Defense policymakers try to balance the demands of a secure defense against the reality of political and financial constraints. There is usually not enough money in the government's budget to obtain all the weapons and personnel that Pentagon planners feel are necessary or would like to have. And even if there were, the expanded military capacity might create new difficulties. An oversupply of arms might arouse other countries' suspicions of hostile

The Joint Chiefs of Staff (JCS) is an advisory group made up of the military heads of each service. In 1987, the JCS consisted of (left to right) General Alfred M. Gray, commandant of the Marine Corps, Admiral Carlisle A. H. Trost, chief of naval operations, General Larry D. Welch, chief of staff of the air force, General Carl Edward Vuono, chief of staff of the army, Admiral William J. Crowe, chairman, and General Robert T. Herres, vice-chairman.

intent; too many tanks and troops on a battlefield could get in each other's way; or taxpayers might complain about how their money was being spent.

These strategic dilemmas have engaged some of the nation's best minds—people who maintain a continuing search for answers. But the questions of defense keep changing, and U.S. defense policy must change with them. More than 200 years ago, the nation's primary defense concerns centered on expelling the British from America and suppressing Indian attacks. Today, the British are our allies, and a host of new foes—the atomic bomb, communism, terrorism—havè replaced the old ones.

The DOD and its military components—the Departments of the Army, Navy, and Air Force—form a complex network of civilian- and military-controlled offices and agencies, all of which are structured to ensure the maintenance of civilian control over the armed forces. At the center of this network are the Office of the Secretary of Defense and the Joint Chiefs of Staff, an advisory group composed of the military heads of each service. This book traces the development of the American armed forces, describes the evolution of the DOD from 1947 to the present, and looks at various defense and foreign policy issues.

A young soldier of the Continental Army in 1776. When the Continental Army was created by Congress in 1775 it lacked adequate funds, supplies, and experienced troops. General George Washington had to supplement his army troops with troops from the colonial militias.

TWO

America's First Armed Forces

Even before there was a United States of America, there was a need for American armed forces. The British colonies that would eventually become the first states of the American nation were initially just isolated villages and townships that were carved out of the rugged wilderness along North America's Atlantic seaboard. To the colonists who settled these British outposts, death and danger frequently lurked only yards beyond their cleared plots of land. The greatest danger came from Indian attacks, but invasion by forces from rival colonies bordering those of the British was also a threat. The French, well established in New France (now Canada), repeatedly raided frontier settlements in New England and New York with the aid of their Indian allies. Moreover, they had constructed a string of forts throughout the Ohio Valley, which connected New France to the French colony of Louisiana in the southwest and threatened the westward expansion of the British colonies. To the south of the British colonies, the Spanish colony of Florida also threatened to encroach on Great Britain's colonial holdings.

Because each of the 13 colonies was governed by an official appointed by the British crown—there was not yet a central, American government—no unified military force existed to come to the colonists' defense. Rather, each colony maintained its own militia, which was based on the British model of a civilian force made up of citizen-soldiers. Every colony required all able-bodied males between the ages of 16 and 60 to report for military training at the county or town seat for a certain number of days per year. Local militia commanders, appointed by the royal governor of each colony or by its colonial assembly (a legislative body selected by the male landholders of each colony to represent the interests of the colonists), would call upon the citizen-soldiers to conduct campaigns against Indians or to provide protection during emergencies. Militiamen were expected to furnish their own weapons, ammunition, and supplies. The commander could draft men—as well as property—if enough volunteers did not turn out. This did not mean that a draftee actually had to serve, however, for he could hire a substitute to take his place.

The citizen-soldiers were summoned to take up arms on numerous occasions during the colonial period, often in response to events that originated on the other side of the Atlantic. The best known of these conflicts was the French and Indian War (1754–63), which was linked to the Seven Years' War that raged between Britain and France from 1756 to 1763. In North America colonial militiamen, British army regulars, and Indians loyal to the British cause clashed with French and Indian troops in a series of battles that ultimately left France defeated. As a result, France was essentially knocked out of the race for a New World empire, forced to cede its holdings in Canada to Great Britain and its colony of Louisiana to Spain. (Spain, which had allied itself with France during the war, lost Florida to the British.)

The war had two significant effects on the American colonies. First, it virtually removed the threat of invasion by Britain's rivals in North America. Second—and perhaps more important from America's standpoint—the war taught the colonists military techniques that would serve them well only a short time later in their struggle for independence from Great Britain. From the British troops the ragtag band of colonial militiamen learned war leadership and discipline: Some of the American Revolution's greatest commanders—among them the young George Washington—apprenticed with top British military officers. From the Indians the Americans learned the tactics and effectiveness of surprise attacks, the use of scouts to track the enemy, and the method of fighting from behind cover instead of in close formation out in the open. But at the end of the war, the citizen-soldiers, like so many Americans who would come after them, were eager to lay aside their muskets and powder for their farming equipment, and the part-time army of civilians was quickly disbanded.

In a 1774 lithograph, Boston colonists tar and feather a British tax agent, while in the background other colonists dump tea from a ship—a reference to the Boston Tea Party of 1773. Colonists strongly resisted British efforts to impose taxes and control trade; as hostility grew, they prepared their militias for combat.

The Struggle Against Britain

By the 1770s, however, relations between the American colonies and the British government had become strained. In 1764, the British Parliament had issued the Revenue Act (also known as the Sugar Act), imposing high taxes on some of the goods the colonists imported, such as sugar, wine, and silk. The following year, the Parliament announced the Stamp Act, which required colonists to purchase special stamps that were to be affixed to printed materials, such as newspapers, pamphlets, and legal documents. Like the Revenue Act, the Stamp Act was intended to pay for the costs of maintaining British troops to defend and protect the colonies. But the act caused such a furor in the colonies, which protested the levying of taxes because their interests were not represented in the British Parliament (American colonists did not elect members to Parliament), that it was repealed in 1766.

The imposition of taxes without representation was not the only factor that drove the colonists to rebellion. Many Americans vehemently protested the Quartering Acts of 1765 and 1766, which required the colonial assemblies to provide supplies and housing for British soldiers. Friction between the two groups came to a head in December 1773, when a band of colonists dumped a cargo of tea leaves into Boston Harbor late one night to protest a British company's monopoly on the import and sale of tea. This act of defiance, thereafter known as the Boston Tea Party, so angered the British authorities that they restricted all shipping to and from Boston until the destroyed tea was

British soldiers fire upon colonial minutemen at the Battle of Lexington on April 19, 1775. The British quickly dispersed the rebels and moved on to the town of Concord, where they defeated another contingent of militiamen at the North Bridge.

paid for. They also limited the powers of the local government in Massachusetts.

It was against the backdrop of these events that the Massachusetts militia began to prepare for an armed revolt in 1774. When the commander of the British garrison in Boston discovered that the rebels were hiding weapons and supplies in the nearby town of Concord, he sent soldiers to seize the cache. As the redcoats approached the village of Lexington on the morning of April 19, 1775, American minutemen—militiamen who promised to respond quickly when called to arms—were waiting for the British at the edge of the village green. After a brief skirmish, the British soldiers dispersed the rebels and moved on to Concord, where they met another contingent of Massachusetts militiamen at the North Bridge. In the battle that ensued came the famous "shot heard round the world" that began the war of independence.

The First American Army

At the outbreak of the American Revolution, Britain was the most powerful and technologically advanced country the world had ever seen. British ships weighed anchor in colonies all over the world and traded in countless ports. By contrast, America in the 1770s was a collection of sparsely populated colonies comprising about 2.5 million people—roughly the number of people who live in the Washington, D.C., area today. The colonies were not completely self-sufficient in food or other necessities, and they had no professional armed forces to speak of—only the locally raised militias consisting of citizens willing to take up arms and band together with their neighbors in times of emergency.

Such was the sorry state of affairs that confronted the Second Continental Congress when it convened in Philadelphia in May 1775 to discuss the impending war with Britain. Fully aware that it could not defeat the world's greatest army with only a haphazard force of colonial militia, Congress established the Continental Army on June 14, 1775. One day later it named George Washington, a veteran of the French and Indian War, as commander in chief of the continental forces. Washington had headed Virginia's militia and, as a well-known politician and plantation owner, could afford to supply his militiamen with money from his own pocket. (For this reason it was common for the wealthiest man in town to command the local militia.)

Congress hoped to raise six companies of riflemen recruited from Pennsylvania, Maryland, and Virginia—about 20,000 men—for its Continental Army. But by March 1776, it had managed to enlist only 9,000 troops. The shortage

In 1781, General Benjamin Lincoln was chosen to head the newly created War Department. During the Revolution, Lincoln had won distinction first as a major general in the Continental Army and later as commander of American troops in the South.

of soldiers was not the only area in which the new Continental Army was deficient. It lacked both adequate funds and supplies, and its troops were inexperienced and subject to only short terms of enlistment. Compared to the full-time professional army of the British, the American troops were undisciplined amateurs for whom military service meant time away from their farms, their businesses, and their families with little monetary compensation.

Washington supplemented his scanty force with troops from the colonial militias, which often undermined Congress's efforts to raise troops by offering to pay soldiers more for enlisting and to subject them to shorter terms of service. The funding of the militias continued to come from private sources and monies appropriated by the colonial (and after the Declaration of Independence in 1776, state) assemblies. The militias provided the Continental forces with a much-needed infusion of manpower and contributed to the war effort in several other significant ways. Local militias coming to the aid of the army were fighting on terrain they knew better than either the Continental Army or the British army and thus gave the Americans a distinct advantage. Furthermore, militiamen returning to their farms and businesses after tours of duty kept the fledgling American economy running—something the loosely organized Continental Congress would not have been able to do on its own.

In June 1776, the Continental Congress created the Board of War and Ordnance to oversee the task of administering and supplying the American army. Originally, five members of Congress comprised this forerunner of today's DOD, but in 1777 Congress changed the board's membership from five legislators to three citizens who were not members of Congress. (The number was raised back to five in the fall of 1778, when Congress expanded the board to include two legislators.) In 1781, Congress established the War Office, which replaced the Board of War and Ordnance. The new department was headed by Benjamin Lincoln, a Massachusetts farmer and former militia commander, who was given the title secretary at war.

The Articles of Confederation, which all of the state legislatures had ratified by March 1781, granted Congress the power to declare war and to raise an army and navy. The document forbade the states from maintaining military forces in times of peace without the consent of Congress and prohibited them from making war except in the event of sudden invasion. The cost of war was to be divided among all the states.

By this time the Continental Army had shed its greenhorn image and had been molded into a disciplined fighting force. Its ranks were peppered with foreign soldiers, among them the Polish nobleman Kazimierz Pulaski and the Prussian army officer Friedrich Wilhelm von Steuben, who, as inspector general of the Continental forces, was largely responsible for the army's impressive turnaround. French aid had also contributed greatly to the army's transformation. In 1778, France had signed a treaty of alliance with the rebel government, promising to send both troops and matériel to bolster the American cause.

The turning point of the war came in October 1781 at the Battle of Yorktown, in Virginia. There, surrounded by a combined force of 9,000 American troops and 6,000 French soldiers, the British forces under General Charles Cornwallis surrendered on October 19. Although Great Britain and the United States would not sign a formal peace treaty until 1783, the American Revolution was essentially won on that day.

The new American government was acutely aware of the dangers a professional standing army of paid soldiers posed to a government ruled by the people. History had produced enough examples of military despotism to make their fears well founded, and the oppressive actions of the regular British army were still fresh in the legislators' minds. So in 1784, against the recommendations of George Washington, Congress resolved to "discharge the troops now in the service of the United States, except twenty-five privates to guard the stores at Fort Pitt and fifty-five to guard the stores at West Point and other magazines, with a proportionate number of officers, no officers to remain in service above the rank of captain." It would take several more years and several more wars before the American government would concede the importance of maintaining a strong system of defense.

The Department of War

The first step toward the creation of a permanent military establishment occurred in 1789, when Congress created the Department of War on August 7. The new department was given executive status—that is, its director, the secretary of war (changed from the previous title secretary *at* war), was directly responsible to the president, who under the recently ratified Constitution assumed the role of commander in chief of the armed forces. General Henry Knox, secretary at war since 1785, continued to hold the post under the nation's first president, George Washington.

The War Department was headquartered at Samuel Fraunces's Queen's Head Tavern at the corner of Great Dock (now Pearl) and Broad streets in New York City. (The seat of the U.S. government was in New York until 1790, when it moved to Philadelphia.) The department was responsible for oversee-

Samuel Fraunces's Queen's Head Tavern served as George Washington's military headquarters during the revolutionary war. The building, which still stands today at the corner of Pearl and Broad streets in New York City, has been restored to its 18th-century design and is now a museum.

ing matters dealing with the defense of the country on land and at sea, for carrying out the government's policies regarding Indian tribes, and for the construction of roadways and improvement of waterways. It also supervised the nation's armed forces, which in 1789 numbered about 800 soldiers and officers.

The formation of a War Department by no means signaled that Americans had overcome their reservations about a professional military force. Members of Congress still feared that a standing army could potentially disrupt the civilian government by force, thus taking away the citizens' choice of representation. Indeed, the memory of the British still haunted the nation's early legislators, so much so that in 1791 Congress passed and the states ratified the Third Amendment to the Constitution, stating, "No Soldier shall, in time of peace be quartered in any house, without the consent of the Owner, nor in time of war, but in a manner to be prescribed by law."

Congress was still firmly convinced that the state militias were the best alternative to a large standing army. The Constitution gave Congress the power to call up the militias to "execute the Laws of the Union, suppress Insurrections and repel Invasions." Congress was also vested with the authority to organize, arm, and discipline the militia and to govern "such Part of them as may be employed in the Service of the United States." Having concluded in the Second Amendment to the Constitution in 1791 that "a well regulated Militia" was "necessary to the security of a free State," Congress passed the Militia Act the following year. The act required all free men between the ages of 18 and 45 to enroll in the militia of their respective states and established enrollment and organization procedures. It left the enforcement of these procedures up to the states, however, which often resulted in anything but well-organized units. At a time when loyalty to one's state was as strong as one's loyalty to the United States, the jealousy the states felt toward each other and toward the new federal government defeated Congress's efforts to regulate the militia beyond a bare minimum. The outcome, for the most part, was an unevenly trained and undisciplined force of limited usefulness in times of military crisis.

The Emergence of the U.S. Navy

From the first days of the Revolution, Americans had banded together to challenge British supremacy at sea. As early as the spring of 1775, almost every colony had makeshift naval forces composed of fishermen, sailors, and traders who harassed British naval ships traveling the waters off the American coast. American privateers—privately owned ships fitted with cannons and authorized by the government to seize goods or people carried aboard enemy vessels—also worked to disrupt the English economy by preying upon British merchant ships.

In November 1775, Congress officially created the Continental navy and marines. Though these naval forces never played a major role in the winning of the American Revolution, the exploits of such leaders as Captain John Paul Jones, considered to be the father of the U.S. Navy, helped cripple the British

The naval exploits of such leaders as Captain John Paul Jones helped cripple the British war effort during the American Revolution. Jones, who was born in Kirkcudbright, Scotland, is considered the father of the U.S. Navy.

war effort. The importance of a navy was not lost on America's leaders, however. French naval forces coming to the aid of their American allies contributed significantly to the defeat of the British at Yorktown. A French fleet under the command of the Comte de Grasse blockaded access to the town by sea and repulsed a British naval attempt to reinforce General Cornwallis. With no means of relief or escape, Cornwallis was forced to surrender.

After the war, the American navy was quickly and completely disbanded. Though the Constitution granted Congress the power to "provide and maintain a Navy," it was not until 1794 that any action was taken to rebuild the navy. That year, Congress commissioned the construction of six ships to protect American merchant vessels from attack by privateers from the Barbary States (now the states of Algeria, Tunisia, Tripolitania, and Morocco), who operated in the Mediterranean Sea. By raiding U.S. ships, these privateers were violating a fundamental principle of the new republic—that of the freedom of navigation, the idea that the ships of all neutral nations should be able to sail freely and without fear of attack on the oceans of the world.

Until 1798, the secretary of war oversaw all land and sea operations of the U.S. military. But as the nation's armed forces grew, the responsibilities of managing the entire military became too much for one person to handle effectively. In April 1798, Congress transferred all naval and marine forces to a new cabinet-level department called the Department of the Navy. Like the Department of War, the Department of the Navy was headed by a civilian secretary appointed by the president and confirmed by the Senate. The first secretary of the navy, Benjamin Stoddert, a Washington, D.C., merchant, began to mold the fledgling navy into a competent fighting force. By the end of 1798, the U.S. Navy possessed 14 ships, and several more were under construction. It appeared at last that Congress was beginning to heed the words spoken by George Washington in 1793: "If we desire to avoid insult, we must be able to repel it; if we desire to secure peace . . . it must be known that we are at all times ready for war."

A Second Test

The American armed forces soon faced their second test in battle. In June 1812, long-simmering animosities between the Americans and the British erupted into the War of 1812. Both the army and the navy saw action in the war, which is sometimes called the "Second American Revolution" because it solidified the United States's sense of independence from European affairs.

Although Great Britain possessed a vastly superior navy (at the time, the British navy had more than 600 vessels, compared with the U.S. Navy's 17), the young American navy performed admirably. Its most significant contributions took place on the Great Lakes, where it dealt the English a series of

On September 11, 1814, an American naval fleet under Commodore Thomas Macdonough defeated a British squadron on Lake Champlain, thwarting British plans to sail down the Hudson River and divide New England from the rest of the United States. The important victory helped sway negotiations then under way in Ghent, Belgium, to end the war.

blows that crippled Britain's war strategy. The last and most important of these showdowns occurred on September 11, 1814, when Commodore Thomas Macdonough and his 16-ship squadron defeated a British squadron on Lake Champlain. Macdonough's triumph prevented the British from advancing down the Hudson River and thwarted their plans to divide the New England region from the rest of the United States.

The role of the U.S. Army in the War of 1812, unlike that of the navy, was less than spectacular. The few troops the army had were poorly trained, ineptly led, and scattered all over the United States. (In 1811, the army consisted of fewer than 3,000 men; by the time war was declared, its troop strength had increased to about 7,000.) Although the British had only 5,000 soldiers and about 1,800 Indians under the Shawnee chief Tecumseh with which to repel an invasion of Canada, the unprepared American army suffered defeat after defeat along the northern U.S. border.

33

The state militias proved to be of little help in the conflict. Three states—Massachusetts, Rhode Island, and Connecticut—refused to send their militias to aid the federal forces because they disagreed with Congress's decision to declare war. During one promising skirmish in October 1812, a group of New York militiamen, claiming that they were obligated only to defend their country and not to invade Canada, would not back up a small force of regular, or professional, soldiers who had moments earlier taken the Canadian bank of the Niagara River. The militiamen watched from the opposite bank as the outnumbered regulars were either killed or captured. And in the summer of 1814, when the militias from nearby states were summoned to repel the British advance on the nation's capital, only 7,000 of the 95,000 men called to arms appeared. The poor turnout enabled the British troops to march on Washington, where they set fire to the Capitol, the White House, and many other federal buildings. The militia somewhat restored its tarnished reputation several weeks later at Fort McHenry, which guarded the entrance to the harbor at Baltimore. The American victory—as symbolized by the battle-scarred American flag that continued to fly atop the fort after the battle—inspired the American lawyer and poet Francis Scott Key to write the words to "The Star-spangled Banner" while imprisoned by the British aboard a vessel anchored nearby. The militia's actions at Baltimore were not enough to erase

A draft of "The Star-spangled Banner" written by Francis Scott Key shortly after the British bombardment of Baltimore in September 1812. Key wrote the words to what would become the country's national anthem while imprisoned by the British aboard a ship anchored near the fighting.

the stigma the group had gained, however, and a rift between the regular army and the state militias (today known as the National Guard) developed that to some extent still exists today.

Despite the less than laudable performance of its ground forces, the United States won the War of 1812. On Christmas Eve, 1814, the two countries signed the Treaty of Ghent, agreeing to end the hostilities. The war precipitated several important changes in the nation's military. The U.S. Navy had held its own against the world's most advanced sea power, and its stunning triumphs did much to alter American perceptions about the necessity of a well-prepared naval force. Soon after the war, the Board of Naval Commissioners, a three-member committee composed of the navy's senior captains, was created to oversee the construction and outfitting of ships, advise the secretary of the navy on shipbuilding programs, and develop plans for better supply and monetary procedures.

The War Department also underwent changes as a result of the war. During the conflict, two distinct groups developed within the army: the staff and the line. The staff was composed of the department's leadership in Washington and included the personnel of such offices as the judge advocate (who handled all matters pertaining to military justice), the paymaster (who was responsible for the distribution of wages), and the inspector general (who oversaw the training of troops). The line consisted of the troops in the field, which belonged either to the infantry, cavalry, or artillery. (This system of line and staff is still employed by the army today.)

In 1815, Congress limited the standing army to 10,000 troops, against the entreaties of President James Madison, who had asked Congress to set the number at 20,000. Most of the 40,000 soldiers who were serving in the army when the war ended were quickly discharged, a pattern that was to be repeated time and again over the years. By maintaining only a skeleton force in peacetime and increasing troop strength only after the outbreak of hostilities, the country was often ill prepared to meet a military crisis. This practice of keeping the military at a minimum at the expense of military preparedness has been debated in Congress since the days of George Washington and still embroils lawmakers on Capitol Hill today.

After the War of 1812, the United States focused its attention on economic growth and westward expansion. Since the early 1800s, the country had more than doubled in size with the purchase of the Louisiana Territory from France in 1803 (whereby the United States gained a vast amount of land between the Mississippi River and Rocky Mountains) and the acquisition of Spanish Florida in 1819. The army played an important role in opening these new regions to

U.S. settlement. First, it helped subdue Indian attacks incited by the ever-increasing numbers of Americans establishing homesteads on land that the Indians had hunted and tilled for thousands of years. From 1815 to the end of the century, the army fought sporadic wars against various tribes in the West and Southeast and was responsible for executing treaties and overseeing Indian affairs until 1849, when the Department of the Interior took over these duties.

The army's second important contribution to the expansion of the United States was made by its growing corps of engineers. The Army Corps of Engineers had been established on March 16, 1802, the same day as the military academy at West Point, New York, where the army engineers received their training. From a small initial number of students the group of civil engineers had steadily increased, much to the benefit of the United States. The country, caught up in a great burst of industrialism, was in need of trained engineers, and many of the army's elite corps were commissioned by private companies to lend their expertise in building the nation's roadways, railroads, and waterways. Among the projects army engineers had a hand in building over the years were the Baltimore & Ohio Railroad (built in the mid-1800s), the

An engraving of Captain Meriwether Lewis and Lieutenant William Clark holding council with Indians. Lewis and Clark led an expedition from 1804 to 1806 to map the Louisiana Purchase and find a route to the Pacific Ocean. This engraving appeared in a book written by Patrick Gass, an army regular, who was a member of the expedition.

Panama Canal (completed in 1914), and the Tennessee Valley Authority's system of hydroelectric dams (constructed between 1933 and 1944). Other members of the corps followed in the footsteps of army captain Meriwether Lewis and his assistant, Lieutenant William Clark, who, with approximately 30 regular soldiers, became the first group of Americans to explore the Pacific Northwest in 1804. Engineers educated at the military academy at West Point surveyed and mapped most of the unchartered territory west of the Mississippi River, opening the way for American settlement of the region.

At the same time army engineers were helping to stretch the western frontier of the United States, U.S. naval ships were seeking to travel farther afield from their home ports. Steam-powered ships had been developed, and the navy was no longer at the mercy of the wind to propel its vessels. Though it saw little military action between 1815 and 1860, the navy was far from idle. At the request of Congress it undertook a number of voyages to explore distant lands or open up U.S. trade. In 1838, for example, an expedition led by navy lieutenant Charles Wilkes set sail for the coast of Antarctica, where its members conducted scientific research, returning to the United States in 1842. Probably the most well known naval expedition of the period, however, was Commodore Matthew Perry's diplomatic mission to Japan in 1853 and 1854. As a result of Perry's negotiations, two Japanese ports, Shimoda and Hakodate, were opened to U.S. trade, thus ending 250 years of Japanese self-imposed isolation from the West. These and other voyages not only served to increase trade and scientific knowledge but also signaled the emergence of the United States as a naval power.

The Mexican War

After a relatively peaceful period of 30 years, the nation again went to war in 1846. Ten years earlier, the territory of Texas had declared its independence from Mexico. Although Mexico was not happy about losing Texas to the Texans, it was livid when it lost the territory to the United States, which annexed the independent republic in 1845. In April 1846, tensions escalated into war when the two sides clashed in southern Texas. The army, unprepared for war, quickly put out a call for volunteers, who were incorporated into the regular army rather than the state militias. General Winfield Scott, a brilliant military tactician and veteran of the War of 1812, was in charge of the assault on Mexico City, Mexico's capital. In March 1847, he landed at Veracruz with about 12,000 troops and began to fight his way inland toward the capital. The

General Winfield Scott, a veteran of the War of 1812, led the American assault on Mexico City in 1847. Though the Mexicans outnumbered U.S. forces by about three to one, Scott's outstanding leadership and daring tactical maneuvers resulted in an American victory.

Mexican force under General Antonio López de Santa Anna outnumbered the Americans by about three to one, but by the time Scott's small army took Mexico City on September 14, 1847, it had been forged into a formidable fighting force.

Though Mexico had no sea forces, the U.S. Navy nonetheless played an important role in the war. Its ships transported army troops to Mexico and blockaded the country's coastlines. Its most outstanding contribution, however, was in the taking of California, which at that time was Mexican territory. A naval squadron ferried from place to place the few army troops assigned to the overwhelming task of bringing the entire territory under U.S. control. This enabled the American forces to subdue the enemy without having to travel hundreds of miles on foot. By July 1846, the Americans captured Los Angeles and Santa Barbara, and California was in U.S. hands.

The Mexican War, which ended in February 1848 with the signing of the Treaty of Guadalupe Hidalgo, was a war of firsts for the U.S. military. It was the first war that was not fought on American soil, and it was the first war in which many of the army's officers were educated at West Point. It was also the first time American troops had exhibited so much discipline and skill in battle. The armed forces had come of age in Mexico, but this new U.S. military would soon face its bloodiest and most trying test as the country was torn apart by the Civil War.

A Nation Divided

While the United States in the mid-19th century was rapidly expanding its military and economic influence throughout the world, tensions between the different regions within the country were also mounting. The urbanized and industrialized states of the North were increasingly at odds with the agrarian states of the South, whose economies were heavily dependent on slavery and cotton. As states and territories were added to the growing country, mutual animosities gradually escalated, and the two sides became engaged in a political struggle over whether the new regions would be designated "slave" or "free." Also, many in the South believed that the individual states should have more control over their own affairs, whereas most people in the North felt that the federal government should have ultimate power over the individual states. It was this hotly contested issue of states' rights that led 11 Southern states to secede from the Union and form the Confederate States of America in early 1861.

The Civil War divided not only the nation but also the nation's armed forces. When war broke out in April 1861, more than 300 of the army's officer corps, among them Robert E. Lee, Joseph E. Johnston, and Pierre G. T. Beauregard, resigned their commissions and offered their services to their home states. (The president of the Confederacy, Jefferson Davis, was a West Point graduate and former secretary of war.) By the time the first shots resounded at Fort Sumter, South Carolina, on April 15, the Confederacy had about 35,000 men in uniform, almost twice the number of soldiers in the U.S. Army. On May 3, President Abraham Lincoln, anxious to get the cumbersome war machinery moving even though Congress was not in session, issued a proclamation increasing the regular army by 22,000 men. In addition, he asked for 42,000 volunteers to enlist for a period of 3 years. He also activated the state militias and placed them under the command of the federal government. As the fighting between the North and the South dragged on, however, these troops were not sufficient to meet the demands of the war. Consequently, in 1863 Congress passed the Enrollment Act, the nation's first draft law. This act, which authorized the president to conscript men between the ages of 20 and 45 into the U.S. Army, was so unpopular that riots erupted in several Northern cities in protest.

The rapid expansion of the nation's ground forces had a corresponding effect on the War Department. An Army Board made up of the heads of the department's offices and bureaus was formed to coordinate army policy and advise the secretary. In addition, three assistant secretary positions were created to help ease the workload on Secretary of War Edward M. Stanton. These changes lasted only for the duration of the fighting, however, and were abolished when the war ended.

Jefferson Davis (seated, third from left), president of the Confederate States of America, meets with members of his cabinet and General Robert E. Lee (standing, center) during the Civil War. Before the war, Davis, a graduate of the U.S. Military Academy, had served as President Franklin Pierce's secretary of war.

On April 9, 1865, Robert E. Lee surrendered to Ulysses S. Grant in this small farmhouse in Appomattox Courthouse, Virginia. Although the peace applied only to the Army of Northern Virginia—and not to the entire Confederate army—Lee's surrender essentially ended the conflict between the North and the South.

Although the brunt of the fighting fell to the U.S. Army, the navy had an important role to play in the conflict. Early in the war, President Lincoln ordered a blockade of all Southern ports. U.S. Navy ships cut off such strategic harbors as Charleston and New Orleans, successfully stemming the exportation of cotton and restricting the import of needed ammunition and other supplies. Also, navy gunboats patrolled Southern rivers and carried out attacks against Confederate forts located along the riverbanks.

On April 9, 1865—nearly four years to the day after war was declared—the two armies made peace at Appomattox Courthouse, Virginia. The Civil War was over. More than 600,000 soldiers had died in the fighting—more Americans than would die in World War I. The Civil War has often been called the first modern war because industrial power and such new technology as ironclad ships, repeating rifles (which enabled soldiers to fire one shot after another without having to stop and reload), telegraph communication, and railroads played a major role in the outcome.

After the war, the United States entered a new era characterized by immense economic and political growth. This period of prosperity and expansionism would witness the emergence of the U.S. Army and Navy as the most powerful military force in the world.

41

The mangled wreckage of the USS Maine lies partly submerged in Cuba's Havana Harbor after the ship mysteriously blew up in February 1898. The blast, which most Americans had attributed to foul play on the part of Spain, plunged the United States into the Spanish-American War.

THREE

Toward a Unified Defense

After the Civil War, the United States again turned its attention away from military matters and focused on economic and political expansion. By 1866 the army, which at its peak in 1865 had numbered more than a million soldiers, was reduced to a fraction of its former size—fewer than 60,000 men. Moreover, these forces were spread thinly across the expanse of the nation. Whereas some were detailed for occupation duty in the South during the Reconstruction period, others defended the long line of the western frontier.

Like the army, the navy was neglected after the war. But as U.S. business interests in foreign countries increased toward the end of the century, the United States began to develop a strong naval force to protect American shipping. In the 1890s, Congress appropriated funds for the development of a battleship force, and the U.S. Navy began to build a modern fleet that could rival the best navies of Europe.

In February 1898, one of the navy's battleships, the USS *Maine*, mysteriously blew up while moored in the harbor at Havana, Cuba. All 260 men aboard were killed in the blast, which most Americans attributed to foul play on the part of Spain. (Many experts today believe that the explosion was caused by a fire in the ship's coal bunker that spread to its ammunition stores.) Cuba, a Spanish colony at the time, was struggling to establish its independence, and American sentiment rested with the Cubans. The slogan Remember the Maine, to hell with Spain! soon echoed across the United States as an outraged American public demanded revenge. By April 1898, the two countries were at war.

The Spanish-American War was, for the most part, a naval war. On May 1, the U.S. Navy won an important victory at Manila Bay, the Philippines, when, in a matter of hours, Commodore George Dewey defeated the Spanish fleet stationed there. One month later, a naval force under Rear Admiral William T. Sampson destroyed another Spanish squadron off the coast of Santiago de Cuba. The victory essentially crushed the Spanish war effort, and on August 12 the two sides agreed to end hostilities.

The war brought changes to both the War Department and the Navy Department. Within the navy, a Strategy Board composed of naval officers was created to advise the secretary of the navy on strategic matters pertaining to the U.S. fleet. Although the board was abolished when the war ended, an outgrowth of this group, the General Board of the Navy, was formed in 1900 to counsel the secretary on such matters as shipbuilding programs, war plans, and general policy.

The army's deployment in the war had uncovered grave problems at the War Department in Washington. As a result of poor organization within the department, food and supplies that were to be shipped to Cuba had been delayed, had been loaded onto the wrong transports, or did not arrive at all. There had not been enough doctors to care for the wounded or the thousands of soldiers who contracted such tropical diseases as malaria and yellow fever. (More than 5,000 soldiers died from disease or other noncombat causes, such as food poisoning, whereas only 379 men died in battle.) The War Department's ineptness in managing the war led Congress to pass the General Staff Act in 1903. Prior to the act, both the commanding general of the army and the separate bureaus of the Department of War reported directly to the secretary of war, with little or no coordination between the groups. Under the new law, which was enthusiastically endorsed by Secretary of War Elihu Root, the position of chief of staff was created to replace that of the commanding general. In addition, the general staff corps, composed of three generals, was established to oversee matters pertaining to administration, planning, and military intelligence and education. The general staff, the troops in the field, and the department bureaus would all report to the chief of staff, who would, in turn, report to the secretary of war and the president.

Two other significant events occurred within the military in 1903. First was the passage of the Militia Act, which mandated that federal dollars be used to

Elihu Root, secretary of war from 1899 to 1904, played a prominent role in convincing Congress to pass the General Staff Act of 1903. The act created the position of chief of staff and established the general staff corps, which oversaw matters pertaining to administration, planning, and military intelligence and education.

help pay for militia training and entrusted responsibility for this training to the army. The Militia Act greatly improved the quality of training among members of the militia (which had been popularly called the National Guard since the late 1800s). Furthermore, joint maneuvers between the federal forces and the National Guard went a long way toward erasing the uneasy feeling between the two groups. The second important event was the creation of the Joint Army and Navy Board, a group of high-ranking officers from both the army and the navy that coordinated joint military activities and planning. The establishment of this board was one of the earliest attempts to integrate the activities of the armed services and foreshadowed the later movement to unify the nation's armed forces.

The centralized command system adopted by the War Department in 1903 soon encountered opposition from both the army and Congress. The bureau heads, disgruntled with having some of their duties usurped by the general staff, complained about their loss of power. Some members of Congress, on the other hand, feared that the department was losing control over the army.

As a result, 13 years after it passed the General Staff Act, Congress rescinded portions of the law by passing the National Defense Act of 1916. This act reinstated the bureau chiefs' right to report directly to the secretary of war and prohibited the general staff from doing any work "that pertains to established bureaus or offices of the War Department." It set the peacetime strength of the regular army at 175,000 soldiers and added 2 new bureaus to the War Department: coast artillery and the National Guard. It also established procedures for mobilizing the National Guard in times of emergency and formally organized the army's components into the Regular Army, the National Guard, and the Organized Reserves (civilian enlisted men and officers available to supplement the Regular Army in the event of war or other emergencies).

The Rise to Power

The National Defense Act was signed into law in the midst of the first great global war—World War I. In 1914, long-standing rivalries among the European powers over colonial expansionism and military supremacy had escalated, and when Franz Ferdinand, archduke of Austria, was assassinated by a Serbian national, Europe exploded into war. Although World War I would ultimately involve 28 countries, the principal participants at the outbreak of the conflict were Britain, France, and Russia on the one side (known collectively as the Allied powers), and Germany and Austria-Hungary on the other.

Though it provided the Allies with munitions and supplies, the United States did not want to be drawn into European affairs, preferring to remain neutral. But when the Germans sank several U.S. ships and tried to convince Mexico to invade the United States, the U.S. government could not maintain this policy of isolationism. In April 1917, it joined the Allied war effort, and for the first time in the history of the United States American soldiers crossed the Atlantic to participate in a foreign war.

To raise troop strength rapidly, Congress enacted the Selective Service Act of 1917. All men between 21 and 30 years of age were required to register for military service, and draftees were chosen by lottery—the first time this type of system was used. Of the approximately 4 million U.S. servicemen who served during World War I, almost three-fourths of them were drafted through the Selective Service Act.

As the U.S. Army expanded to meet wartime needs, so did the War Department in Washington. But the departmental changes of 1903 and 1916 had not solved the problems of disorganization and inefficiency. Competition

*In 1918, a blindfolded woman in Atlanta, Georgia, chose a capsule contain-
ing a draft number and then handed it to Secretary of War Newton D. Baker
(in civilian clothes), who officially opened the capsule. To raise troop strength
rapidly during World War I, Congress passed the Selective Service Act of
1917 and, for the first time in U.S. history, a lottery was used to determine
who went to war.*

between the general staff and the department bureaus still existed, and often
the actions of the personnel in Washington actually worked against each other.
In 1918, the department was again reorganized to help remedy some of the
problems. The chief of staff was given more control over the bureaus, and the
heads of the various committees of the general staff received greater authority
over their areas of responsibility. However, the reorganization failed to resolve
old tensions between the chief of staff in Washington and the overall army
commander in the field. Although the commander of the American forces in
Europe, General John J. Pershing, was supposed to convey his opinions and
recommendations to the president and the secretary of war via the chief of
staff, he frequently reported directly, bypassing the chief of staff entirely. This
not only added to the confusion at the War Department but also fostered
resentment between the chief of staff and the general commander.

The navy did not play a major role in World War I, nor was it afflicted by
departmental disorganization to the extent that the army was. After navy

personnel had repeatedly urged that officers be given more influence over the day-to-day operations of the U.S. fleet, the navy had finally established the position of chief of naval operations in 1915. However, the commander who filled this post had much less control over naval affairs than his army counterpart had over army affairs. He was closely supervised by the secretary of the navy and had no authority over the department's bureau heads.

World War I forever intertwined the U.S. military with events in the rest of the world. By the war's end in November 1918, the United States had risen to prominence as a world power. Now expected to assume a leadership role, it would no longer be able to shy away from global issues. The war also saw the advent of many new military technologies, such as the tank, the machine gun, long-range artillery, and poison gas. It was the first time that airplanes had been used in combat, and the army's fledgling aviation unit had its first taste of battle.

Army artillerymen during World War I prepare a 155-millimeter howitzer, a type of cannon, for action. World War I saw the advent of many new military technologies, including long-range artillery, the tank, the machine gun, and poison gas.

The postwar period was also the first time since the creation of the American armed forces that Congress authorized more than a skeletal troop strength in peace. Under the National Defense Act of 1920, the maximum size of the U.S. Army was set at about 17,700 officers and 280,000 enlisted men. In addition, the act created three new branches within the War Department—the Air Service, the Chemical Warfare Service, and the Finance Department—and gave the chief of staff four assistants. The following year, General Pershing took over as army chief of staff and proceeded to organize the general staff into five divisions: personnel and administration, military intelligence, operations and training, supply, and war plans.

With the increasing complexity of the military and America's new responsibilities as a world power, Congress began to seriously consider consolidating the armed forces under one department. Between 1921 and 1945, it examined more than 50 proposals on the unification of the military. In 1922, the armed forces moved a step closer to this end when they created the Army and Navy Munitions Board to coordinate the purchase and use of war matériel in the hopes of lowering defense costs. Both the army and the navy strongly opposed most efforts at unification, however. They were afraid that if the two departments were combined, they would lose the power to act independently of each other. And both branches of the military had struggled too long and fought too hard to get where they were to want to concede any of their autonomy. But as much as they fought the idea, the services were doomed to lose. Time and experience would prove the value of a unified military establishment, and the event that decided the issue was World War II.

World War II

By 1939, the U.S. Army was ranked 18th in the world in troop strength, just after Portugal. But this was soon to change. In September 1939, Germany invaded Poland, and the European countries again divided against each other. Germany, Italy, and Japan allied to form the Axis powers. Britain, France, Russia, and China joined forces as the Allied powers.

As it had in World War I, the United States tried to remain neutral. But on December 7, 1941, Japanese planes attacked the naval base at Pearl Harbor, Hawaii, and the United States could no longer watch from the sidelines. Once the country entered the war, the U.S. military rapidly eclipsed both its enemies and allies alike in size and matériel. From a troop strength of 267,000 in 1940, the U.S. Army grew to more than 8.2 million in 1945. Similarly, the navy increased from 161,000 to more than 3.3 million over the period. By the end of the war in September 1945, the United States had become the greatest military power the world had ever known.

With this massive buildup of troops came problems for the U.S. military. The U.S. armed forces not only had to coordinate the many varied activities of their own naval, air, infantry, artillery, armored, motorized, and support divisions; they also had to organize activities with other nations' forces. Congress responded to this need for better organization by passing the War Powers Act of 1942. This act reduced three divisions of the army's general staff—personnel and administration, operations and training, and supply—and created three major commands: the Army Ground Forces Command, which was responsible for training the combat troops of the ground forces; the Services of Supply Command (later renamed the Army Service Forces), which encompassed the administrative, logistical, and technical elements of the army; and the Army Air Forces Command, which was given authority over the training, personnel, and supply of the army's air forces. These new commands reported directly to the army chief of staff, George C. Marshall. As the military head of the army, Marshall was a member of the newly formed U.S. Joint Chiefs of Staff (JCS), which had been created in February 1942 to advise the president on military matters relating to the conduct of the war. Joining Marshall on the JCS were Admiral Ernest J. King, the chief of naval operations, and General Henry H. "Hap" Arnold, the commanding general of the Army Air Forces. Under the direction of the president, these three men were responsible for drafting war plans, implementing strategy, allocating forces, and managing the war in general.

The JCS also met with the British Chiefs of Staff (who, along with the JCS, formed the Combined Chiefs of Staff) to develop and oversee strategies that involved the troops of several nations. Perhaps the best example of the military's need for large-scale planning and coordination was the massive Allied invasion of the Normandy coast of France in the spring of 1944. For two months prior to the June 6 invasion, known as D day, American and British pilots bombed railways, airfields, and bridges in France. On the night before D day, paratroopers were dropped behind enemy lines to cut German communications, and a fleet of Allied ships off the French coast bombarded the area. The following morning, tens of thousands of British, Canadian, and U.S. troops under General Dwight D. Eisenhower crossed the English Channel in 5,000 Allied boats and stormed the Normandy beaches. By July 1, nearly a million troops had been landed. The success of the Normandy invasion, which was the largest amphibious operation in history, was probably the climactic

General George C. Marshall (seated, center), chief of staff of the army from 1939 to 1945, meets with members of his staff to discuss military operations during World War II. Marshall was one of the first members of the military to advocate the unification of the services into a single department.

event of World War II. It not only turned the tide against Nazi Germany but also proved that the conduct of complex, multifaceted military operations could and should be an integral part of defense planning.

The Debate over Unification

Even before the massive undertaking at Normandy, the upper levels of America's military leadership had seen a need for greater coordination between U.S. air, sea, and ground segments. As early as 1943, General Marshall had endorsed administrative unification. The following year, as the Normandy invasion was just getting under way, the army submitted a proposal before the House Select Committee on Post-War Military Policy for the creation of a Department of the Armed Forces. According to the plan, the department would be headed by a single civilian secretary who would serve as the primary adviser to the president on political, economic, and administrative issues that pertained to the U.S. military establishment. Three civilian under secretaries representing the army, air force, and navy would aid the secretary in his duties. The proposal retained the concept of the JCS and expanded the group to include an overall chief of staff in addition to the heads of the services. The navy, however, still opposed the idea of a unified military establishment and strongly urged the House committee to study the issue further. The committee agreed with the navy's recommendation in its June 1944 report, and several more studies were undertaken by various branches of the military.

The first of these was conducted by the Special Committee for Reorganization of National Defense, commissioned by the JCS. In April 1945, the four-member committee, chaired by Admiral James O. Richardson, recommended a plan (although Admiral Richardson opposed it) to establish a Department of the Armed Forces with a civilian secretary as its head. Unlike the proposal submitted to the House committee in the spring of 1944, the JCS study did not provide for civilian officials to head each service. Furthermore, it recommended that all the armed forces come under the supervision of a single commander, who would also serve as military chief of staff to the president. The commander of the armed forces would be aided by a general staff and the commanders of the individual armed services. The secretary, the commander of the armed forces, and the commanders of the individual armed services would make up the U.S. Chiefs of Staff, which would advise the president on military strategy and defense spending. As before, the navy rejected the proposal, fearing that unification would result in the downgrading of its forces.

Another plan submitted to the Senate Committee on Military Affairs in late 1945 combined components of the JCS and the earlier army studies. This plan, also proposed by the army, called for a Department of the Armed Forces to be headed by a civilian secretary. An under secretary and three assistant secretaries—one for scientific research, one for legislative affairs and public information, and one for procurement and industrial mobilization—would assist the secretary. A chief of staff of the armed forces, chosen from among the military and responsible to the secretary of the armed forces, would direct the nation's armed services. In addition, the army, navy, and a separate air force would each be headed by a chief of staff, who would be subordinate to the chief of staff of the armed forces. Together, the service chiefs, the chief of staff of the armed forces, and the president's chief of staff would form the U.S. Chiefs of Staff. This group would be responsible for advising the president on military matters via the secretary of the armed forces.

Although this plan had the backing of both the army and the air forces, the navy was still quite reluctant to lend its approval. It adamantly opposed the idea of placing the armed forces under the command of a single chief of staff. By doing so, it contended, the military balance achieved by maintaining separate service departments would be destroyed, and civilian control could be usurped.

It was also afraid that it would be forced to surrender its aviation units to the newly proposed air force and to relinquish the Marine Corps to the army.

By this time, however, the navy realized that some sort of coordinated military organization was inevitable. In September 1945, it issued its own proposal, which was known as the Eberstadt report after Ferdinand Eberstadt, a former chairman of the Army and Navy Munitions Board who headed the study at the request of Secretary of the Navy James V. Forrestal. In keeping with the navy's reluctance to relinquish any of its autonomy, the Eberstadt report recommended maintaining three "coordinate departments" for the army, navy, and air force rather than creating a single military department encompassing all of the armed services. It also concluded that the navy should retain its air wing. In a different approach from the army proposals, it recommended the formation of a National Security Council to help formulate

In 1945, Ferdinand Eberstadt, a former chairman of the Army and Navy Munitions Board, headed a task force commissioned by Secretary of the Navy James V. Forrestal to study the concept of military unification. Eberstadt's report recommended the creation of a National Security Council to advise the president on issues pertaining to defense and national security.

President Harry S. Truman optimistically informs Army Air Forces general Carl Spaatz, Secretary of War Robert P. Patterson, and Secretary of the Navy James V. Forrestal of his goal to unify the military services into one department in this cartoon that appeared in the Washington Evening Star *on January 18, 1947. One month later, Truman sent legislation for the creation of a unified department to Congress and, on July 25, Congress passed the National Security Act, providing for the cabinet-level National Military Establishment.*

policy and advise the president. The council would be made up of the president—who would serve as chairman—the secretaries of state, war, navy, and the air force, and the head of the proposed National Security Resources Board, an organization that would advise the president on the coordination of military, industrial, and civilian mobilization. Finally, to coordinate activities between the branches of the military, Eberstadt recommended retaining the JCS and creating several joint committees and agencies.

In December 1945, President Harry S. Truman took matters into his own hands, sending a proposal to Congress for the creation of a Department of National Defense. "One of the lessons which have most clearly come from the

54

costly and dangerous experience of [World War II]," he said, "is that there must be unified direction of land, sea and air forces at home as well as in all other parts of the world where our Armed Forces are serving." Truman's plan called for the department to be headed by a civilian secretary of national defense. Each of the three "coordinated branches" of the military—army, navy, and air force—would be headed by an assistant secretary. Each branch would likewise be headed by a military commander, who would report to a military chief of staff. The three service commanders and the chief of staff would serve as an advisory group to the secretary of national defense and the president.

In proposing this unified defense establishment, Truman wished to integrate the military's strategic plans, merge its military program and budget, cut defense expenditures, foster coordination between the military and other government agencies, and establish strong civilian control over the military. Though the army and the navy still could not agree on the issue, the president continued to pursue unification. While Congress debated the proposal during the spring and summer of 1946, Truman further refined his ideas about the new military department. Instead of three assistant service secretaries as originally proposed, he now supported separate civilian secretaries for the navy, air force, and army. Each of these service secretaries would report to the secretary of national defense, who would be a member of the president's cabinet. Although the air force would be separated from the army and made an individual branch of the military, the navy would be allowed to keep its air units. The Marine Corps would likewise remain under the navy's jurisdiction.

By the beginning of 1947, the army and navy had finally reached an uneasy compromise on unification. On February 26, President Truman sent legislation for a single military department to Congress. Throughout that spring, Congress conducted lengthy hearings on the proposed bill. Both the Senate and the House finally passed the bill, known as the National Security Act, on July 25. One day later, while en route to his dying mother's bedside, President Truman signed the act aboard the presidential plane, and the U.S. military organization entered a new phase.

In the 1950s, crewmen review their orders before carrying out a training mission in a B-52 bomber, one of several types of aircraft that make up the air force's Strategic Air Command (SAC).

FOUR

The Modern Era

The National Security Act of 1947 was the most significant legislation to affect the U.S. military since the creation of the War and Navy departments in the late 1700s. The act completely reorganized the nation's armed forces, combining all the existing services under a single cabinet-level organization called the National Military Establishment (NME). The Department of the Navy, the Department of the Army (as the War Department was now called), and the newly created Department of the Air Force continued to exist within the NME as individual executive-level departments. (The Marine Corps remained a service within the navy.) Although grouped under one organization, the service departments retained considerable autonomy. Each was to be headed by a civilian secretary responsible for administering the affairs of his or her respective department.

According to the legislation, the "general direction, authority, and control" of the entire NME would be in the hands of the secretary of defense, who, like the individual service secretaries, would be a presidentially appointed civilian confirmed by the Senate. The role of the secretary of defense would be to establish "general policies and programs" for the NME, to "take appropriate steps to eliminate unnecessary duplication or overlapping in the fields of procurement, supply, transportation, storage, health, and research," and to "supervise and coordinate the preparation of the budget estimates."

Members of the National Security Resources Board convene in August 1950. The board, one of several agencies created by the National Security Act of 1947, was established to advise the president regarding the coordination of military, industrial, and civilian mobilization. It was abolished in 1953.

In addition, the National Security Act legally recognized the JCS as "the principal military advisers to the President and the Secretary of Defense" and designated its membership as the chiefs of staff of the army, navy, and air force as well as the chief of staff to the commander in chief, a senior military officer who reported to the president. Among the responsibilities assigned to the JCS were preparing strategic plans and directing strategic military operations, establishing unified commands (commands made up of the forces of two or more service departments), developing joint strategies for the supply and deployment of the nation's armed forces, determining policies for coordinated training exercises and military schooling, and reviewing the personnel and weaponry needs of the services.

Several new agencies were established under the National Security Act to strengthen national security and to aid the president in his new role as a leader in the world political arena. The National Security Council (NSC), first proposed by the navy in 1945, was created to advise the president on "the integration of domestic, foreign, and military policies relating to the national security so as to enable the military services and the other departments and agencies of the Government to cooperate more effectively in matters involving the national security." Seven members would make up the council: the president, who would serve as presiding officer, the secretaries of state, defense, army, navy, and the air force, and the chairman of the newly formed National Security Resources Board. In addition, the president could designate other members with the approval of the Senate.

Another agency established by the National Security Act was the Central Intelligence Agency (CIA). The successor to the Office of Strategic Services, which had been formed in 1942 and then disbanded shortly after World War II, the CIA concentrated on the foreign-intelligence needs of the executive branch. Its primary responsibilities were to organize, assess, and distribute information concerning national security, coordinate the intelligence-related activities of government departments and agencies, and advise the NSC on these activities.

Finally, the National Security Act established three other organizations: the War Council, the Munitions Board, and the Research and Development Board. The first of these, the War Council, was charged with advising the secretary of defense "on matters of broad policy relating to the armed forces." It was

An atomic bomb is detonated at Bikini atoll in 1946 to measure the effects of an underwater nuclear blast on U.S. ships. The atomic bomb, with its unprecedented potential for mass destruction, forever changed the way military and political leaders thought about war and international relations.

composed of the three service secretaries, the three service chiefs of staff, and the secretary of defense, who acted as chairman. The Munitions Board took over the duties of the Army and Navy Munitions Board and coordinated the department's activities regarding the purchase of equipment and matériel. The Research and Development Board succeeded the Joint Research and Development Board, which had been created in 1946 to foster and oversee research and development programs for the military.

Facing New Challenges

As sweeping and comprehensive as the National Security Act of 1947 was, however, it was inadequate to deal with the rapidly changing political situation of the postwar world. Even the most farsighted of America's policymakers had trouble keeping up with the frenzy of events that followed the close of World War II. Long before the war ended, most astute policymakers had recognized that the United States would emerge with newfound influence as a result of the economic destruction of the traditional European powers. Some, too, had foreseen the rise of the Soviet Union as a threat to the democratic countries of the West. Although the Soviet leader, Joseph Stalin, had promised to hold democratic elections in the Eastern European countries the Soviet Union occupied after the war, by 1947 most Americans realized that Stalin had no intention of living up to his word. A feeling of mutual suspicion developed between the two countries as a result of these political tensions. This intense distrust gave shape to what is known as the cold war, when the United States and the Soviet Union conflicted over ideological differences and fought each other with espionage and hostile propaganda rather than with arms.

The cold war and America's responsibilities as a superpower were not the only factors that influenced military and foreign policy in the wake of World War II. The use of the atomic bomb on Hiroshima and Nagasaki in August 1945 forever changed the way military and political leaders thought about war and international relations. This new weapon, unprecedented in its destructive power, created new challenges for both civilian and military decision makers responsible for the security of the United States. A question of primary importance was how the atomic bomb, which threatened to make all other weapons obsolete, would be controlled.

In response to all of these new challenges, the U.S. government embraced a policy of maintaining the international status quo by preventing the further spread of Soviet-style communism. This policy, known as containment, was originally outlined in 1947 by George Kennan, a director of the State Department's policy planning staff and later a U.S. minister to the Soviet Union, in his "X Article," thus named because it was published anonymously in the journal *Foreign Affairs*. Containment, as explained by Kennan, sought to "confront the Russians with unalterable counterforce at every point where they

Secretary of Defense James V. Forrestal reviews an army honor guard in Heidelberg, Germany, in 1948. A former secretary of the navy, Forrestal saw the DOD through its tumultuous first years, when interservice rivalries hindered the effectiveness of the new department.

show signs of encroaching upon the interests of a peaceful and stable world." By doing so, the United States hoped to relax the exercise of Soviet power.

In military terms, containment meant accumulating enough firepower to restrain the Soviets from expanding into other parts of the world—as well as preventing an attack on the United States. Technological improvements in communications and transportation made the world a smaller place, especially in the event of a crisis. If America were forced to fight a war again, it would have much less time to train and mobilize new troops. For this reason, Truman's advisers argued, the United States would need a well-stocked arsenal of nuclear bombs.

But at the same time that his advisers were advocating a buildup of weapons, Truman was trying to cut defense expenditures. After World War II, the majority of Americans called for a reduction in the amount of federal dollars spent on defense. Truman, facing an election campaign in 1948, was eager to give the people what they wanted. To solve his seeming dilemma of lowering defense costs while maintaining adequate defense measures, Truman turned to James V. Forrestal, the nation's first secretary of defense.

Defense Policy Under Secretary Forrestal

As secretary of the navy during World War II, James V. Forrestal had vigorously opposed the unification of the armed forces. The deed was done, however, and Forrestal readily accepted President Truman's offer in 1947 to fill the nation's highest defense post. He was faced with the monumental job of translating the government's foreign policy into military terms and molding the NME into a cohesive department. This in itself was no easy task, as interservice rivalries still riddled the military. These squabbles, coupled with divergent priorities and reduced budgets, preoccupied the department for the first few years of its existence.

An advocate of low defense spending during peacetime, Secretary Forrestal was charged with devising a defense budget that would be both affordable and acceptable to the president. This often required skills akin to tightrope walking, as President Truman, ever sensitive to public opinion, demanded budget cuts, whereas the services, bent on military one-upmanship, lobbied for more money. Each of the services had its own pet project that it wanted to see supported. The army, for instance, wanted universal military training for all males over the age of 18, whereas the navy wanted a fleet of large aircraft carriers and the air force wanted to expand its fleet of fighters and bombers.

They could not all have their way, and it often fell to Forrestal to smooth the military chiefs' ruffled feathers.

The incessant infighting between the services led Forrestal to call two special conferences with the JCS in 1948 in an attempt to settle their differences and further define the roles of the individual services. Among the questions that still had not been settled was which branch of the military would be responsible for the control of nuclear weapons. This issue was somewhat resolved at the second of the conferences convened that year, which was held at the Naval War College in Newport, Rhode Island, from August 20 to 22. At this meeting, the NME's top leaders agreed that the air force would have primary responsibility for carrying out strategic bombing involving nuclear weapons. The navy, however, would also have access to nuclear weapons and would not be excluded from conducting strategic air campaigns.

By the beginning of 1949, Forrestal had been in office long enough to realize that the National Security Act did not go far enough in unifying the military. Ironically, the man who had been one of the strongest opponents of unification now found himself urging the president to propose an amendment that would strengthen unity between the military departments. On March 5, 1949, Truman sent a proposal to Congress to amend the National Security Act. Five months later, on August 10, Congress acceded to the president's wishes by passing Public Law 216.

Under these amendments, the NME was renamed the Department of Defense and given executive status, meaning that the department was now directly responsible to the president. The army, navy, and air force departments, on the other hand, lost their status as executive departments and were downgraded to military departments. In addition, the service secretaries were removed from the NSC, leaving only the secretary of defense to represent the military on the council. The law further clarified the role of the service secretaries, stating that the military departments were to be "separately administered by their respective Secretaries under the direction, authority, and control of the Secretary of Defense." A deputy-secretary position and three assistant secretaries were added to the Office of the Secretary of Defense. Finally, the JCS was expanded to 4 members to include a nonvoting chairman, and the Joint Staff was increased from 100 to 210 officers.

The 1949 amendments to the National Security Act were a major step toward attaining real unity in the military. Removing the separate services from participation in the NSC prevented them from making their appeals directly to the president. Without a direct role in defense policy-making, the services would be compelled to work together under the secretary of defense.

The Revolt of the Admirals

Though Forrestal had worked hard to bring the 1949 amendments to reality, he was not around to see them put into effect. Having resigned in March 1949 for health reasons, he was replaced by Louis A. Johnson, a former assistant secretary of war and Truman's chief fund-raiser in his 1948 election bid. An outspoken leader, Johnson was committed to Truman's objective of lowering defense expenditures and attacked the matter almost immediately upon taking office. One of his first moves was to cancel construction of the navy's supercarrier *United States*, which touched off a storm of protest from the navy and brought about the immediate resignation of Secretary of the Navy John L. Sullivan.

Louis A. Johnson, secretary of defense from March 1949 to September 1950, is pictured in his office at the Pentagon. An outspoken and controversial leader, Johnson canceled construction of the navy's supercarrier United States *shortly after taking office, a move that touched off a storm of protest from navy personnel and prompted a House investigation.*

The ensuing dispute, often referred to as the "revolt of the admirals," was the first test of the secretary's new power. Though Johnson had the backing of the majority of the JCS, the navy charged that he had acted without consulting members of the navy. Navy personnel lashed out at the secretary by questioning the effectiveness of the air force's B-36 bomber and accused Johnson and Secretary of the Air Force W. Stuart Symington of contract fraud and conflict of interest (Johnson had sat on the board of directors of the company that manufactured the plane) in acquiring the plane. In an investigation of the navy's charges, the House Committee on Armed Services found no evidence of misconduct on the part of Johnson and Symington, though it did question the army and air force chiefs' ability to comment on the needs of the navy. It also reprimanded Johnson for his decision to cancel the project without consulting Congress, saying, "National defense is not strictly an executive department undertaking; it involves not only the Congress but the American people as a whole speaking through their Congress."

The First Postwar Test

On June 25, 1950, soldiers from Communist North Korea invaded U.S.-occupied South Korea, and the DOD was put on a war footing for the first time since unification. Though the strength of the U.S. armed forces had been pared down to comply with Truman's budgetary demands, the military was more prepared to respond than usual, thanks in large part to the Selective Service Act that Congress had approved two years earlier. The act required all men between the ages of 18 and 25 to register for the draft and set the length of service at 21 months.

As a result of the war, Truman's defense-budget ceilings were removed. Also gone was Secretary Johnson. In September 1950, Truman, displeased with the controversy that seemed to plague Johnson's tenure, had asked his defense secretary to step aside. In his place, Truman appointed former army chief of staff George C. Marshall. Marshall was highly respected for both his wartime leadership role and his excellent diplomatic skills as secretary of state after World War II.

The first big test of the DOD's military effectiveness came in September 1950. General Douglas MacArthur, the supreme commander of the U.S. and UN troops in Korea (the United Nations had sent in a multinational force shortly after the North Koreans had overrun South Korea), had devised a brilliant but risky plan that would utilize all of the armed services. Marines and soldiers, supported by naval and air bombardment, would conduct an amphibious landing at the coastal town of Inchon, along the western coast of South Korea. From there, MacArthur's forces would launch a campaign inland to recapture the South Korean capital of Seoul. If successful, the plan would crush the North Korean army, concentrated in the south of the country, by choking off its supply lines. The invasion had to be extremely well planned, because tidal changes at Inchon allowed landing craft to land for only a few hours three days a month. If there were any snags, the whole operation would be in jeopardy.

The invasion went off as planned on September 15, and by the end of the month MacArthur's forces had retaken Seoul. Two weeks later, the entire North Korean army had been run out of South Korea. The U.S. military machine had passed its first test with flying colors.

By 1951, however, the war had reached a stalemate. Chinese troops, coming to the aid of the Communists, had poured into North Korea and halted the South Korean advance. Both President Truman and Secretary Marshall wanted to seek a diplomatic end to the fighting, but General MacArthur

General Douglas MacArthur, the supreme commander of U.S. and UN troops in Korea, greets his commander in chief, President Harry S. Truman, during a conference on Far Eastern policy held at Wake Island in October 1950. Six months after the meeting Truman relieved the World War II hero of all his commands for publicly disagreeing with the president's policies to end the Korean War.

advocated launching an all-out offensive in North Korea. When MacArthur publicly challenged his commander in chief's decision, Truman, supported by Marshall and the JCS, relieved the World War II hero of all his commands, sending a loud message to both the military and the American public that civilians were firmly in command of the nation's armed forces.

Eisenhower's "New Look" in Defense

By the time the Korean War ended in 1953, the nation had a new president and a new secretary of defense. Dwight D. Eisenhower, the mastermind behind the Normandy invasion of France during World War II, was now in the White House. The former army general chose Charles E. Wilson, a native of Ohio who had directed General Motors' defense production effort during World War II, as his secretary of defense.

Eisenhower's approach to defense spending, like that of his predecessor, was based on his desire for a balanced national budget. He referred to his vision of U.S. defense policy as the "New Look." It called for equipping the armed forces as efficiently as possible and for streamlining the administrative structure of the Defense Department. This policy, known in shorthand as "more bang for the buck," emphasized the deterrent and destructive power of nuclear weapons, the superior ability of America's bombers and missiles to reach their target, and an effective air-defense system. The rationale behind the New Look was that if the use of nuclear weapons was a viable option from the outset of a conflict, then a smaller and less expensive conventional defense structure could be maintained. Although the New Look did not rule out the maintenance of conventional ground, naval, and air forces, it saw nuclear warfare as a sort of bargain-basement defense.

This approach brought forth a new concept in U.S. military thinking, the doctrine of nuclear superiority, or U.S. supremacy in terms of the number of nuclear bombs the country possessed and the explosive power these bombs contained. Such superiority was thought to be valuable for America's ability to intimidate potential enemies and to give it a superior bargaining position in a crisis—in other words, to deter an enemy from taking any military action against it.

The nature of the New Look caused tensions between the services to boil over. Lower defense budgets meant that some—or all—of the services would not receive the funds they had hoped for and planned on getting. The constant jockeying between the chiefs of staff for the president's favor and a bigger

Members of the Joint Chiefs of Staff in the JCS conference room at the Pentagon in November 1952. They are (left to right): General J. Lawton Collins, chief of staff of the army, General Hoyt S. Vandenberg, chief of staff of the air force, General Omar Bradley, chairman of the JCS, and Admiral William M. Fechteler, chief of naval operations. During the early 1950s the JCS were frequently at odds with one another on how to spend the money budgeted for the military services.

share of the defense budget infuriated President Eisenhower, who thought that the joint chiefs were still too interested in protecting partisan service interests to administer a truly national defense policy. He wanted the JCS to be strictly a strategic planning and advising agency, not a unit of command. In military terms that meant that the JCS members would be *staff* as opposed to *line* officers.

In April 1953, Eisenhower sent a plan to Congress calling for the reorganization of the DOD. Under the plan, the joint chiefs of the respective services would be responsible to the service secretaries for efficiency and combat readiness. To further increase efficiency and economy at the DOD, Eisenhower recommended abolishing four agencies within the department, including the Research and Development Board and the Munitions Board, and creating in their place six additional assistant secretary positions (for a new total of nine). Each assistant secretary would be responsible for a certain function—for example, manpower or research and development—and would review defense programs on a continuing basis and help the secretary institute improvements in the execution of these programs.

The result of Eisenhower's reorganization plan, which took effect on June 30, 1953, was a pyramid-shaped power structure with the secretary of defense at the top. All information, commands, authority, and communications issued from the Office of the Secretary of Defense. Under the secretary were the nine assistant secretaries and the JCS, which, apart from the individual chiefs' responsibilities to the service secretaries for combat readiness, had no day-to-day command of the services. The assistant secretaries and the JCS served as the principal advisers to the secretary of defense. Upon receiving their counsel, the secretary then issued orders to the unified commands (for example, the Pacific Command, which is made up of personnel from all of the services and which is responsible for the defense of the Pacific theater) and the three service secretaries.

These organizational changes helped unify the chain of command, but they did not completely resolve the problems within the department. In 1958, a study conducted by the Rockefeller Brothers Fund, a philanthropic organization, recommended further changes to "correct the inefficiency and duplication of effort growing out of interservice rivalry." That August, Congress passed the Defense Reorganization Act of 1958, which gave the secretary of defense added power, including the authority to "assign, or reassign, to one or more departments or services, the development and operational use of new weapons or weapons systems" and the right to establish agencies to carry out "any

In 1958, Nike Ajax missiles, which are capable of carrying either nuclear or conventional warheads, are poised to strike in the event of a Soviet attack. By the late 1950s, land-based and sea-based nuclear weapons joined air-based weapons as the three main elements of U.S. nuclear defense.

supply or service activity common to more than one military department." In addition, the JCS replaced the service secretaries as the agents responsible for conveying the secretary of defense's orders to the unified and specified commands (commands headed by a single service but that serve the needs of the entire military, for example, the Strategic Air Command, which is an air force command that is responsible for the control of America's nuclear bombs and intercontinental missiles). The JCS chairman was also given voting privileges, and the Joint Staff was increased to a maximum of 400 officers.

By the late 1950s, the United States had developed long-range land-based and sea-based missiles capable of carrying nuclear warheads. These new missile systems joined nuclear bombs as the main elements of U.S. nuclear

70

defense, forming what came to be called the strategic triad. For more than 30 years, this triad would continue to be America's greatest insurance against nuclear attack.

The McNamara Years

During his successful campaign for the presidency in 1960, John F. Kennedy warned of a missile gap that had grown dangerously lopsided in the Soviet Union's favor. Although it was later determined that the missile gap never existed—that the United States consistently had more missiles in its arsenals than the Soviet Union had throughout the 1950s and 1960s—Kennedy strove to build up the U.S. inventory of nuclear and conventional weapons and launched an ambitious space program independent of the military.

The Kennedy defense policy was largely the brainchild of Robert S. McNamara, Kennedy's choice as secretary of defense. A former president of the Ford Motor Company, McNamara applied the highly successful principles of management and economics that he had used at Ford to the DOD. His corporate managerial style, though it successfully pinpointed duplication and financial excesses in the military, was controversial among the military chiefs because his conclusions often did not concur with their opinions. Throughout his tenure, McNamara dictated budgets, force structure, and sometimes even weapons systems without much regard for the advice of his military chiefs, a practice that added to the already strained relationship between the DOD's civilian leadership and its military command.

McNamara supported the concept of deterrence and gave voice to the policy of assured destruction (later known as mutual assured destruction), by which he meant that the United States's capacity to inflict an "unacceptable degree of damage" after a surprise attack by the Soviet Union would deter the Soviets from using nuclear weapons. Unlike his predecessors, McNamara also supported increasing the number of conventional combat troops. He believed that the Soviet Union would try to engage the United States in small regional wars fought through secondary countries that reflected the ideals of the United States or the Soviet Union rather than risk a direct attack on America or its NATO allies. This meant that the armed forces had to be sufficiently prepared and adequately staffed to respond to minor outbreaks anywhere in the world—something the civilian leadership under Truman and Eisenhower had refused to consider because of the budget increases that a troop buildup would

The McNamara Style at Work

Robert S. McNamara was born in San Francisco on June 9, 1916, and began his career in the 1930s as an instructor at the Harvard Business School. He specialized in applying statistical analysis—the collection and evaluation of data to uncover trends and aid in decision making—to management problems. During World War II he served as part of a team of U.S. Army Air Forces systems analysts who determined what the army needed to conduct its bombing campaigns by breaking each raid down into its component parts and studying each part separately. These "whiz kids," as they came to be called, drew up detailed plans for all aspects of the Army Air Forces' bombing missions in Asia: among other things, the number of pilots and crewmen needed; the number and type of aircraft to be used; the number of missions required; the anticipated deaths and casualties; and the quantities and technical requirements for the bombs that were to be used. The whiz kids' techniques were spectacularly successful, and after the war McNamara and his co-workers were hired by the Ford Motor Company to increase the company's efficiency and profitability. Here McNamara was so successful that in November 1960 he became the first company president who was not a member of the Ford family. But only five weeks after gaining that coveted position,

Defense Secretary McNamara holds a Pentagon news conference in 1963 to discuss savings of a billion dollars in the DOD procurement program.

he left Ford to become President John F. Kennedy's secretary of defense.

To McNamara, the analytical approach to defense policy ensured sound, confident decision making. One of his most notable innovations at the Defense Department was the Planning-Programming-Budget-ing System (PPBS). Before McNamara took over as secretary, the Joint Chiefs of Staff would arrive at a figure for the upcoming year's defense budget by looking at the strategic threat to the United States in the context of worldwide commitments and then requesting force levels to meet this threat. Each chief of staff determined his department's projected budget figure without consulting the other services, and this often resulted in duplication and wasteful spending. The JCS would submit its proposal to the secretary of defense, who would then submit it for congressional approval. After Congress had allocated the defense funds, the secretary would divide the available resources among the military departments.

McNamara introduced a new phase between the two steps—that of programming. He asked his systems analysts in the Office of the Secretary of Defense to perform objective evaluations of the Joint Chiefs' requests. As a result, the JCS would have to compare alternative methods of meeting national security objectives. The secretary's decision about which programs to include in the budget proposal would then be based on the cost effectiveness of the various methods considered.

The service departments did not like this intrusion upon their autonomy. They argued that by its nature, cost-benefit analysis could not place a value on intangible qualities that contribute to the effectiveness of the military, such as morale, courage, and leadership. Nonetheless, McNamara applied his system to many areas of the defense budget, especially to weapons development. Among the programs he canceled was the air force's B-70 bomber, which was slated to replace the B-52 bomber and which, he contended, was unnecessary and too costly. Although McNamara reported that his methods saved the government $14 billion between 1961 and 1965, his success at reducing defense costs did not always receive the enthusiastic support of Congress. Many lawmakers on Capitol Hill strenuously objected when his cost-cutting decisions affected jobs in their states and districts.

Though controversial, McNamara's methods did regulate the DOD's budget process and helped prevent wasteful duplication of manpower and resources among the services. For instance, before McNamara introduced cost-benefit analysis at the DOD, the air force and the navy had not bothered to coordinate their nuclear strategies. But perhaps the best testament of McNamara's success is that the decisions he made and the procedures he initiated at the Pentagon are still used to a remarkable extent today.

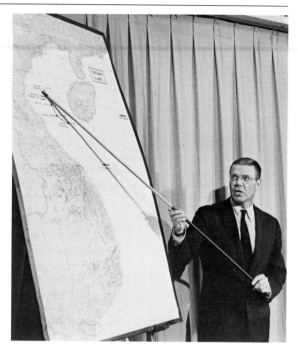

On August 5, 1964, a day after two U.S. destroyers were allegedly attacked by the North Vietnamese in the Gulf of Tonkin, Secretary of Defense Robert S. McNamara announces that U.S. naval aircraft are carrying out retaliatory raids on North Vietnam. After the North Vietnamese attack, Congress issued the Tonkin Gulf Resolution, supporting the U.S. raids and authorizing the president to undertake any other "necessary" military measures.

require. Between 1961 and 1962, the U.S. armed forces increased by more than 300,000 troops. The number then leveled off until 1965, when the United States sent combat troops to defend the American-backed government of South Vietnam.

Managing the War in Vietnam

America's military involvement in Vietnam started long before the first U.S. combat troops landed there in the mid-1960s. As early as 1950, President Truman had sent military advisers to that country, which, like Korea, had divided into a Communist north and a non-Communist south after World War II. During the 1950s, only a few hundred American advisers were in Vietnam at any one time, but in the 1960s, as the situation heated up, the number began to increase. When two U.S. ships allegedly were fired on by the North Vietnamese in the Gulf of Tonkin in August 1964, President Johnson pressed Congress to act quickly to authorize the bombing of the North and the dispatch of 100,000 American troops to help defend the South. (Testimony heard after the Gulf of Tonkin incident suggests that the original version of the story was not altogether true; more than a few experts hold that the second ship was not fired upon at all but that the "attack" was actually caused by stormy weather and rough seas.) Members of the JCS were unanimous in their support of the bombing and urged President Johnson to continue the attacks, which they felt would bring about a speedy resolution of the hostilities. None felt that a war using ground troops could be won easily, if at all. Fearful of the adverse public opinion that increased bombing might cause, Johnson chose to take the middle ground—neither committing the United States wholeheartedly to the war nor completely disengaging it from the conflict. As the situation in Vietnam deteriorated, the JCS pressed Johnson to call up the reserves and fully mobilize for war. But the president did not act on his military chiefs' advice, choosing instead to continue to send troops to Vietnam in piecemeal fashion.

By early 1968, as public opposition to the war mounted, both Johnson and Secretary McNamara had developed grave doubts about whether the war could be won. Disillusioned, McNamara left office in February 1968 and was replaced by President Johnson's close friend Clark M. Clifford, a Washington, D.C., lawyer. In March, President Johnson announced that he was taking steps to turn the fighting over to the South Vietnamese army. At the same time, he announced that he would not seek another term as president. The task of pulling U.S. troops out of Vietnam would fall to Richard M. Nixon and his first secretary of defense, Melvin R. Laird.

The Nixon-Laird Years at the Pentagon

Whereas McNamara had been the supreme analyst in the Pentagon, Melvin Laird was the supreme politician. Nixon had won election in 1968 with a promise to end the war in Vietnam. He chose Laird, an eight-term member of the House of Representatives with experience in defense matters, to help heal the wounds of the war.

Laird gave himself four years to accomplish four goals: to remove American forces from Vietnam; to restore self-respect and confidence to the military; to lower the defense budget; and to reform the draft. He was less interested in national security in a global context than McNamara had been but was popular with the professional military because of the deference he showed its leaders—despite the major budget and force reductions he instituted. He successfully pressured the services to promote women officers and once

Melvin R. Laird, President Richard M. Nixon's first secretary of defense, announces the withdrawal of 50,000 troops from Vietnam in December 1969. Laird made the removal of troops from Vietnam his top priority.

rejected the navy's entire promotions list for rear admiral because there were no women on it. By the time he left office in January 1973, there were nine women generals and admirals in the U.S. armed forces, the first ever to have attained the ranks.

Schlesinger Takes Command

In July 1973, James R. Schlesinger took over as secretary of defense when Elliot L. Richardson, Laird's successor, was appointed attorney general. A strategist, Schlesinger felt that budget cutting under Laird had gone too far and was eroding force readiness. He responded to the growing Soviet military strength by beefing up NATO's conventional forces and revising strategic nuclear doctrine to account for the fact that the Soviets could now match the

United States almost missile for missile. He disagreed with McNamara's doctrine of mutual assured destruction, saying that it would only lead to the destruction of the American population. Instead, he developed a counterforce policy intended to minimize retaliatory damage by targeting Soviet military installations, rather than Soviet cities, in the hopes that the Soviets would refrain from attacking U.S. cities.

The Post–Nixon Era at the Pentagon

With the election of President Jimmy Carter in 1976, Harold Brown took over as secretary of defense. A physicist by training and secretary of the air force during the McNamara years, Brown proposed organizational changes to streamline and better integrate the DOD's operations. In October 1977, Congress passed legislation that incorporated the majority of his recommendations, most significantly the elimination of one deputy secretary of defense (there were two at the time) and the creation of two under secretaries of defense—one for policy and the other for research and engineering. In 1978, Brown introduced further changes at the DOD, reducing the number of assistant secretaries from 22 to 16 and initiating the proposal to admit the commandant of the Marine Corps to the JCS. (Previously, the commandant was allowed to attend only those meetings regarding matters in which the Marine Corps was involved; he did not have full voting privileges.)

Standing Tall at the Pentagon: Reagan and Weinberger

When Ronald W. Reagan became president in early 1981, one of his top priorities was to reverse the perceived weakness of the U.S. military under Carter. Reagan acted quickly to strengthen U.S. military might by proposing large budget increases. His secretary of defense, Caspar Weinberger, had earned the nickname "Cap the Knife" because of his drastic budget-cutting measures (particularly in the area of defense) as director of the Office of Management and Budget during the Nixon administration. Despite this history, Weinberger submitted huge increases for a peacetime defense budget, securing funds for such ambitious programs as a 600-ship navy and the Strategic Defense Initiative (SDI), or "Star Wars" defense system, the aim of which is to destroy incoming nuclear missiles in space.

Secretary of Defense Caspar Weinberger (right) and Secretary of State George Shultz (left) appear before the Senate Armed Services Committee in April 1983 to present a request by President Reagan to deploy MX missiles in existing silos in Wyoming and Nebraska. During his seven-year tenure as secretary, Weinberger requested unprecedented increases for a peacetime defense budget and gained funding for such ambitious programs as the Strategic Defense Initiative.

As commander in chief, Reagan deployed American troops on several occasions during his eight-year tenure in office. In 1982, he sent marines to Lebanon as part of a multinational peacekeeping force to patrol the strife-torn capital of Beirut. A year later, on October 23, a lone terrorist crashed his bomb-laden truck into the marines' temporary barracks at the Beirut airport, killing 241 U.S. servicemen. Only two days after the bombing in Beirut, Reagan dispatched troops to the tiny Caribbean island of Grenada to help quell an uprising by Marxist rebels. America's intervention there was brief, however, and by December 24 all U.S. forces had been recalled. During 1987 and 1988, President Reagan sent a small fleet of ships to the Persian Gulf when fighting between Iran and Iraq threatened to cut off shipments of oil out of the gulf. The U.S. ships escorted oil tankers in and out of the war zone, thus keeping the sea lanes open and assuring the free flow of oil.

In October 1986, President Reagan signed the Goldwater-Nichols Department of Defense Reorganization Act, the first major restructuring of the DOD in almost 30 years. The act, which took its name from the two legislators, Senator Barry Goldwater and Congressman Bill Nichols, who shepherded the bill through Congress, established the chairman of the JCS as the principal military adviser to the president, secretary of defense, and the NSC—a role previously filled by the entire JCS. (However, the individual chiefs could still submit their advice when they disagreed with the chairman or when the president, secretary, or NSC requested it.) The chairman also assumed all of the functions that had been carried out by the JCS as a whole. In addition, the act created the position of vice-chairman of the JCS to assist the chairman and take over in his absence. Although the vice-chairman was allowed to participate in all JCS meetings, he was accorded voting privileges only when acting as chairman. The act also affected the Joint Staff, increasing it from 400 to 1,627 military and civilian personnel.

Budget Cuts Under Bush

In 1989, as the U.S. deficit reached almost $150 billion, President George Bush committed himself to paring down the defense budget. Bush and his defense secretary, former Wyoming congressman Richard Cheney, sought to reduce spending by eliminating or cutting back several projects already in the works, such as production of the navy's F-14 fighter plane and the Marine Corps's V-22 Osprey aircraft. But Congress protested that Bush's cutbacks did not go far enough and targeted such expensive—and technologically controversial—programs as the SDI and the B-2 Stealth bomber, a radar-evading plane, for further cuts. Furthermore, it reinstated funds for some of the programs Bush had cut, including the F-14 fighter program, which prompted Secretary Cheney to comment that the House Armed Services Committee "on occasion funded local interest at the expense of national interest."

At a cost of $550 million apiece, the B-2 Stealth bomber is the most expensive aircraft ever produced. Much of the 1990 budget debate in Congress centered on the radar-evading plane, which many lawmakers believe is too expensive and technologically controversial.

FIVE

The Pentagon's Organization

The Department of Defense is composed of five major divisions: the Department of the Army, the Department of the Air Force, the Department of the Navy (which includes the U.S. Marine Corps), the Joint Chiefs of Staff (JCS), and the Office of the Secretary of Defense. Although it is the military services that carry out the country's defense during time of war, it is the Office of the Secretary of Defense and the JCS that plan, direct, and coordinate the total defense effort. The secretary of defense and the JCS are ultimately responsible to the president, who, as commander in chief of all military forces of the United States, has the final say in any military matter.

All that pertains to the upkeep of each service branch—for example, training, exercises, discipline, and maintenance—is decided and executed by the secretary of that service branch. The secretary of defense is involved in overseeing each service branch in that he represents the needs of all the service branches before Congress and to the rest of the executive branch. But the use of military force (whether in peacetime or in time of crisis) and any decisions that affect all of the services belong to the secretary of defense and his primary military advisers, the JCS.

The Military Services

The army, navy, and air force are responsible for organizing, training, supplying, and equipping their own military personnel for assignment to service commands (groups of units, equipment, or personnel headed by a commander). There are commands for every function the armed forces perform: combat, operations, training, logistics (the distribution of supplies), communications, and matériel (the development and purchase of all kinds of military equipment and supplies).

The service departments are equal in legal and organizational standing to each other but answer to the higher authority of the JCS and the Office of the Secretary of Defense. Each of the departments is separately organized under its own secretary, who is a civilian nominated by the president and approved by the Senate, and a military chief of staff. The civilian secretary is responsible for day-to-day administration and long-range planning from Washington, where he can represent his service branch to the rest of the DOD as well as communicate the secretary of defense's wishes back to his service. In their administrative role, the service secretaries give instructions to their military chiefs of staff. The military chief of staff is responsible for advising the service secretary regarding the service's military needs and seeing that the service secretary's instructions are carried out in the field where troops are stationed.

The first leg of the chain of command runs from the military chief of staff to the geographic commands in charge of all forces of that service in a given area. For example, all of the army forces in the United States (excluding Hawaii and Alaska) take their orders from the Forces Command in Fort McPherson, Georgia. From the geographic commands the chain of command goes to the "higher formations" of the services: the corps and numbered armies of the U.S. Army, the task forces and numbered fleets of the U.S. Navy, the numbered amphibious (land and sea) forces of the U.S. Marine Corps, and the numbered air wings of the U.S. Air Force. From there orders go to the "basic units" of the services: companies, battalions, brigades, and divisions of the army and marines; ships, air squadrons, flotillas, and carrier wings of the navy; and the squadrons and wings of the air force.

The Joint Chiefs of Staff

As the highest-ranking uniformed officer in each military service, the chief of staff works to execute the training, supply, and equipment policies formulated

In October 1989, army general Colin L. Powell became chairman of the JCS. Powell, who had served as President Reagan's national security adviser from late 1987 to early 1989, is the first black to hold the post.

by his service's civilian secretary. He issues orders to the rank and file of military personnel under his command to help him accomplish these goals. The military chiefs of staff serve the DOD as a whole through their work as the JCS and are all appointed to the group by the president with the approval of the Senate for four-year, nonrenewable terms.

The National Military Command Center at the Pentagon, where senior defense officials direct worldwide military forces in times of emergency.

The membership of the JCS consists of the chiefs of staff of the U.S. Army and the U.S. Air Force, the chief of naval operations of the U.S. Navy, the commandant of the Marine Corps, and a chairman and vice-chairman—six members in all. The chairman and vice-chairman are each selected from one of the services but have no single service responsibility of their own. The chairman of the JCS, nominated by the president and confirmed by the Senate, holds the rank of general or admiral and outranks all other officers of the armed services. He serves a two-year term that may be renewed once. The chairman presides over the meetings of the JCS, prepares the agenda, and supervises the Joint Staff, which numbers about 1,600 people. He serves as the principal military adviser to the president, the NSC, and the secretary of defense and offers his expertise in matters such as planning the budget and purchasing military equipment. Although the chairman of the JCS might be an admiral of the U.S. Navy, for example, he tries to speak with one voice for all the military departments.

The vice-chairman, also appointed by the president and approved by the Senate, performs all functions assigned by the chairman and acts as chairman in his absence or when the chairman is unable to carry out his duties because of illness. The vice-chairman participates in all meetings held by the JCS but has no vote except when acting as chairman. He also holds the rank of general or admiral and outranks all other officers in the armed forces except the chairman. The JCS and the staff members who work in their headquarters make up the immediate military staff of the secretary of defense. In addition, the military chiefs of staff keep the civilian secretaries of their services fully informed on matters considered or acted upon by the JCS.

Another role of the JCS is to oversee the operation of *unified* and *specified* military commands in the field. Unified commands are forces made up of two or more service branches working together and controlled by a single commander from one of the services. Six of the eight unified commands are defined by the geographic area in which they operate: European, Central, Pacific, Atlantic, Southern, and Space. The other two, Special Operations and Transportation, are defined by their functions. These joint, multiservice commands control the use of forces; for example, a navy command would receive its operational orders not from the chief of naval operations but from one of the joint commands, which may or may not be headed by a naval officer. The two specified commands are headed by a single service branch but serve the needs of the entire defense establishment under functional categories: The air force's Strategic Air Command consists of all the long-range bombers and land-based intercontinental missiles the U.S. possesses in order to deter a nuclear attack, and the U.S. Army Forces Command organizes, equips, and ensures the combat readiness of all continental U.S. ground units, including the army reserve and the National Guard.

The Office of the Secretary of Defense

The Office of the Secretary of Defense oversees the work of 13 separate defense agencies, each defined by its functional specialization: communications, nuclear weapons, the SDI, national security, investigations, logistics, advanced research, intelligence, mapping, legal services, contract audits, foreign security

Secretary of Defense Richard Cheney appears before the House Armed Services Committee in April 1989 to outline proposed cuts to the 1990 defense budget.

assistance, and on-site inspection (which monitors Soviet compliance with the Intermediate-range Nuclear Forces Treaty of 1987). Each agency is headed by a director appointed by the secretary of defense.

As an executive-level department, the DOD is responsible to the president, and the secretary of defense is a member of the president's cabinet. He or she is appointed by the president and is confirmed by the Senate. Theoretically, the secretary of defense acts as the president's chief adviser on all matters of defense and national security, but in reality a president may rely a good deal more on his national security adviser, other cabinet members such as the secretary of state, or on trusted outside experts. The secretary of defense may not necessarily be the best source of advice because he is usually chosen by the president not for his defense expertise but rather his management or political abilities. But the system is thought to be working smoothly if the secretary of defense has ready access to specific defense expertise from Pentagon personnel whose knowledge and insights the secretary can share with the president.

Besides his role as adviser to the president, the secretary of defense is a member of the NSC along with the secretary of state, the secretary of the Treasury, the national security adviser, the director of the CIA, the president, and the vice-president. Just as the president is the most important individual decision maker in the executive branch, the NSC is the most important advisory body in defense and national security areas. Thus, the national security adviser, who is the permanent chairman of the NSC and the head of its permanent staff, wields considerable influence with the president on issues pertaining to defense.

The Pentagon's Bureaucratic Web

As head of the largest executive department—indeed, one of the largest organizations of any kind—with more than 3 million people on its payroll, the secretary of defense formulates and executes defense policy with the help of a deputy secretary, 2 under secretaries, and 12 assistant secretaries.

The deputy secretary of defense serves as the secretary's chief assistant, acting with the secretary's full authority in emergencies. The under secretary of defense for acquisition oversees the purchase or design and manufacture of everything from hammers and coffeepots to tanks and aircraft carriers. The under secretary of defense for policy represents the department in matters that are outside the Pentagon's immediate purview but nonetheless relate to its work: national security, foreign policy, intelligence, arms-limitation negotiations, the use of outer space, and participation in NATO programs.

Twelve assistant secretaries handle the following areas: special operations; legislative affairs; international security policy; health affairs; force management and personnel; international security affairs; command, control, communications, and intelligence; public affairs; production and logistics; the departmental budget; program analysis and evaluation; and reserve affairs. Other top officials include the general counsel, who is the Pentagon's chief legal officer, and the inspector general, who investigates charges of corruption in the department.

The Divisions of the Pentagon

The National Military Establishment, as the Defense Department was known between 1947 and 1949, had three operational boards in addition to its divisions of the army, navy, and air force: the National Security Resources Board, the Munitions Board, and the Research and Development Board. They were primarily concerned with developing and procuring military equipment and supplies, but over the years the duties of those boards grew enormously. They were therefore abolished and their responsibilities channeled into 12 agencies: the Advanced Research Projects Agency, the Strategic Defense Initiative Organization, the Defense Security Assistance Agency, the Defense Contract Audit Agency, the Defense Communications Agency, the Defense Mapping Agency, the Defense Logistics Agency, the Defense Intelligence Agency, the National Security Agency/Central Security Service, the Defense Investigative Service, the Defense Legal Services Agency, and the Defense Nuclear Agency. Each of the agencies is under the supervision of a director, usually a military officer, who reports to the secretary of defense or one of his top assistants.

The Advanced Research Projects Agency, created in 1958, is involved in basic (theoretical) and applied (practical) research in such areas as computers and semiconductor (a substance having an electrical resistance somewhere between that of electrical insulators and conductors, often used in electronic components and circuits) design. The Strategic Defense Initiative Organization is involved in "Star Wars" research to develop space-based defensive weapons. The Defense Security Assistance Agency handles arms transfers to foreign countries and directs military-aid programs in foreign countries. The Defense Contract Audit Agency provides financial advice to all Pentagon divisions

Lieutenant General James Abrahamson, the director of the Strategic Defense Initiative Organization, displays part of a model of the Strategic Defense Initiative (SDI) while testifying before a Senate appropriations subcommittee in March 1987. The organization carries out DOD research pertaining to "Star Wars" technology.

involved with procurement contracts and evaluates the acceptability of costs claimed or proposed by defense contractors.

The eight other agencies are devoted to single facets of national defense. The Defense Communications Agency develops and maintains the communications systems that are crucial to the coordination of forces, supplies, intelligence, and nuclear forces. The Defense Mapping Agency devotes itself to the provision, on a continuing basis, of complete, reliable, and effective maps for use by military forces. The Defense Logistics Agency procures, maintains, and transports all manner of supplies and personnel to worldwide military outposts.

There are two intelligence agencies under the control of the Pentagon: the Defense Intelligence Agency (DIA) and the National Security Agency/Central Security Service (NSA/CSS). The DIA supplies the secretary of defense and the JCS with regular, worldwide foreign intelligence on military affairs. The NSA/CSS conducts specialized intelligence, communications security, cryptography (code writing and code breaking), and computer-security functions for many sensitive branches of the government, including the CIA and the Federal Bureau of Investigation (FBI), as well as other Pentagon agencies.

The Defense Investigative Service acts as an in-house "FBI" for the Pentagon; it conducts all security investigations and clearances of Defense Department personnel. The Defense Legal Services Agency provides legal advice and services to the Office of the Secretary of Defense and Pentagon agencies.

The engine of a Pershing missile is destroyed in compliance with the 1987 Intermediate-range Nuclear Forces (INF) Treaty between the United States and the Soviet Union. The destruction of the missiles is the responsibility of the On-Site Inspection Agency, which was created in 1988 to carry out the terms of the INF Treaty.

The Defense Nuclear Agency maintains the national nuclear weapons stockpile and the associated reporting system. Much of the agency's work has a "doomsday" quality to it: procedures to respond to nuclear weapons accidents, research on the ability of people to withstand nuclear radiation, and research on the effects of nuclear weapons on military systems.

A 13th DOD agency, the On-Site Inspection Agency, was created in 1988 to carry out the terms of the U.S.-Soviet Intermediate-range Nuclear Forces Treaty of 1987. It is responsible for sending U.S. inspectors to witness the destruction of Soviet missiles and escorts Soviet inspectors on similar missions in Western Europe and the United States.

The Pentagon's Relationship with Congress

A vitally important aspect of the Defense Department's work is maintaining and nurturing its relationship with Congress. The Pentagon can plan its force levels, develop new weapons, and make up schedules for where, when, and how many troops are to be deployed to a certain region, but without Congress to appropriate funds for the activities that these plans represent, the effort is for naught.

Congress is especially important to the Pentagon during the budget process. The budget process begins when Defense Department officials submit a proposed budget to the Office of Management and Budget (OMB), which is part of the executive office of the president. The OMB considers all the executive-branch departmental budget proposals before preparing the nation's overall annual budget. The budget committees of the Senate and the House of Representatives review the OMB document, then pass authorization and appropriation bills, which specify how much money each department will actually get. The Pentagon's total budget for fiscal year 1989 was $290 billion, or approximately 27 percent of the total federal budget.

Although the Defense Department is financially dependent on the budget and appropriations committees, it keeps in closest contact with the Senate and House Armed Services Committees, which have primary oversight over all Pentagon activities. In addition, the Pentagon works with congressional subcommittees that oversee areas ranging from veterans' affairs and intelligence to telecommunications and military construction.

Open missile silos on the USS Sam Rayburn, *a nuclear-powered ballistic-missile submarine. The United States takes extraordinary precautions to en-sure that its nuclear weapons can never be used without the express authority of the president.*

SIX

The Pentagon in the Nation's Service

The Pentagon controls a wide variety of activities ranging from traditional concepts of preserving the national security to sponsoring innovative scientific research to assisting other nations with rural-reform programs.

The DOD, as a cabinet agency, cooperates with the other departments of government in an ongoing process that does not always result in the smooth interaction of agencies. In performing its role as the primary guarantor of U.S. security, the Pentagon often steps into the bureaucratic territories of other government agencies. This is particularly true in the areas of diplomacy and foreign policy, which are ostensibly the sole domain of the State Department. The State Department is charged with conducting the nation's diplomatic relations and overseeing the distribution of foreign-aid dollars (excepting military aid, which the Pentagon handles), but the types of decisions that the State Department is called upon to make quite often entail important considerations of national security.

Many people have called the implicit link between diplomatic and military considerations a fault of U.S. foreign policy. These critics believe that letting security concerns dictate diplomatic decisions has led to the support of foreign governments whose values and policies are counter to American values. Yet there are many others in the U.S. government who argue that in a dangerous world, America's interests must be given top priority over trying to impose the United States's notions about moral behavior on foreign leaders. This friction between practical defense considerations and moral values in foreign policy is an enduring issue in U.S. politics.

Keeping the Military Under Control

Whether in peacetime or in war, one of the greatest concerns of the United States is ensuring that its military is kept under strict civilian control. Assuring that the military abides by the wishes of its civilian leaders is vitally important because there are many examples of other countries in which military leaders have overthrown the legitimate civil authorities.

Since Roman times, the military has traditionally had its own set of rules and regulations, which is known as military law. These laws are different in peace and war, but several traits are nearly constant and universal: laws against desertion, disobeying orders, and being absent without leave (known as going "AWOL"). In times of war, this list would include civil crimes committed by military personnel, such as theft. Some offenses may be punishable by execution. The army, navy, and the air force each maintain a Judge Advocate General Corps made up of both military and civilian lawyers who provide legal services to military personnel and their families. The senior officer of each service's corps, the judge advocate general, supervises all matters relating to military justice. A military trial, called a court-martial, is adjudicated by a jury of military officers rather than by a civil-court judge and jury.

On a larger and more important scale, the Constitution gives Congress the sole authority to declare war. Congress last did this in 1941, after the Japanese attack on Pearl Harbor. But Congress's right to declare war has not stopped various presidents, acting as commander in chief, from involving the United States in several "unofficial" wars—notably in Korea and Vietnam—that were not specifically authorized by Congress. Congress did, however, tacitly approve these ventures by authorizing funds to conduct them.

In response to this ambiguous division of authority, Congress passed the War Powers Act of 1973—over President Nixon's veto—in order to "insure that the collective judgment of both the Congress and the president will apply to the introduction of United States Armed Forces into hostilities." Under the provisions of the law, the president may deploy American forces abroad in hostilities or situations where "imminent involvement in hostilities is clearly indicated" without consulting Congress. However, this authority extends for

U.S. Marines patrol a bomb-shattered street in Beirut, Lebanon, in 1982 as part of a multinational peacekeeping force. President Reagan deployed the marines under the War Powers Act of 1973, which enables a president to send troops into combat without congressional approval but requires that consent after a 60-day period.

only 60 days before specific congressional approval is required for further action.

Although it clarified some gray areas, the War Powers Act introduced new ambiguities. For example: Precisely whom in Congress must the president consult? Precisely when does the 60-day "clock" start, and who has the authority to start it? Congress started the clock on President Reagan twice, when he sent troops to Lebanon in 1982 and during the Grenada invasion in 1983. (In the former case, Congress granted the president an 18-month extension.) Reagan and other presidents since World War II have claimed that in a military emergency there is no time to consult with Congress and, furthermore, that sending military forces to a foreign country is not necessarily a "war" that requires a formal declaration. And presidents since Richard M.

Nixon have suggested that the War Powers Act is unconstitutional on the grounds that it violates the separation of powers of the executive and legislative branches of government. Critics of the act say that it weakens the president's treaty agreements (such as the nation's defense commitments to NATO), but to date no one has formally challenged the law before the Supreme Court. Until that happens, the War Powers Act remains Congress's primary defense, tenuous as it is, against a presidential seizure of its constitutional right to declare war.

Money Matters and Defense Dilemmas

One of the justifications for the enormous expenditure of public funds for defense is that the nation requires unimpeded access to foreign markets and resources. This time-honored notion of national security is often known as the principle of freedom of navigation—that the United States and any other nation has the right to traverse international waters and trade wherever in the world it wants to, without foreign intervention.

Traditionally, however, the best reason for maintaining a strong defense has been the "peace through strength" argument, otherwise known as the theory of deterrence. This theory is summed up simply in an ancient Roman saying: If you want peace, prepare for war. Deterrence is rooted in the belief that the purpose of military might is to prevent a potential conflict before it begins—in other words, to win by not having to fight in the first place as opposed to trying to win after a fight has started, the traditional goal of amassing armed might. The wisdom of this theory, say its supporters, is that it has long been observed that the *threat* of force can be much more persuasive to a potential adversary than the actual *use* of force.

This concept has been the formula for peace—or at least "nonwar"—in Europe since World War II. Neither the United States nor the Soviet Union actually expects that a nuclear war can be confined to Europe, but the idea is that the possibility of using nuclear weapons will outweigh any potential benefits of starting a conventional war. What good is waging war over a territory if war transforms that territory into a radioactive wasteland?

The drawback of this paradoxical notion, according to its detractors, is that much effort and expense must be put into producing military goods and services that have no real purpose in a peacetime context—that is, as long as deterrence is successful in keeping the peace. Each dollar that the U.S. government spends on defense means a dollar not spent on other priorities.

A convoy of American ships escort a Kuwaiti oil tanker through the Persian Gulf during the Iran-Iraq war in 1987. The United States sent a naval fleet to the area when Iran threatened to attack the ships of neutral countries, thus violating the important principle of freedom of navigation in international waters.

This is a familiar economic dilemma with which all governments must wrestle. It is known as the trade-off between guns and butter—guns being symbolic of military spending and butter representing consumer and other public needs.

Many Pentagon critics have argued that the two are incompatible, that defense spending inevitably degrades a nation's standard of living. These same critics argue that the postwar economic success of Japan and West Germany stems in large part from their freedom from the burden of large defense expenditures. The critics contend that governments should work together to enact the conversion of their permanent war economies into nondefense-related production.

On the other hand, there is a longer tradition of defense economics that says that military spending is a necessary component of economic progress, noting that it contributes to full employment and technological advances. Part of the evidence of this is that after the Korean War the rapid decline of the U.S. defense budget was accompanied by stagnation of the domestic economy. Countries that subscribe to this theory—especially small countries such as Israel and Taiwan—seek to recoup their defense expenditures by exporting the weapons they make. However, in the case of large, powerful countries

97

such as the United States, Great Britain, and the Soviet Union, the expenditure of large amounts of money on the military is more often done for political motives rather than for economic reasons.

From a military standpoint, the advent of the nuclear age, with its supersonic bombers and missiles, ensures that there will be no time to mobilize for war once it begins. Therefore, forces-in-being—the military resources in existence at any given time—will be the most important factor in determining a nation's military strength. With forces-in-being now the standard measure of strength, a full-time defense industry must be maintained to produce military goods. (Conversely, until World War II, nations would commonly wait until hostilities broke out before converting factories to war production).

The price of a well-funded defense is economic dependence on the production of war-related goods. It has been calculated that as many as 70 percent of all American engineers work directly or indirectly in the defense industry. According to government figures, for each civilian employed directly by the Defense Department, there are about six others who work in defense-related industries, either as military contractors, suppliers, or con-

---

In 1988, a technician at the Grumman Aircraft Corporation in Bethpage, New York, assembles part of a U.S. Navy aircraft. Towns such as Bethpage, which rely heavily on DOD contracts for economic survival, would suffer serious dislocation if their defense factories were shut down or production slowed as a result of a cut in the DOD's budget.

sultants. Such company towns as Marietta, Georgia (home of a Lockheed Aircraft facility, which builds the air force's SR-71 and U-2 reconnaissance planes), and Bethpage, New York (the home of Grumman Aircraft, manufacturer of the navy's F-14 fighter plane), would suffer serious economic dislocation if their defense factories were shut down or production was slowed as a result of a cut in the Pentagon budget.

Because of the economic dependencies that defense spending can create in towns all over the country, congressmen will go to great lengths to preserve weapons production and prevent the closing of military bases in order to defend the economic livelihood of their home state. Rockwell International, the primary contractor for the B-1 bomber, is said to have helped get congressional approval for that high-cost project by pointing out that subcontractors for the plane were located in 48 of the 50 states.

Arms Control

It is commonly agreed that if a nuclear exchange ever took place between the superpowers, it would be a catastrophe. So why, then, do the United States and the Soviet Union spend billions of dollars on weapons that they cannot even use without threatening the existence of the entire planet? This is the central paradox that may never be resolved as long as nuclear weapons exist, which may be forever, because such weapons of mass destruction cannot be "uninvented."

Neither nuclear weapons nor conventional weapons can be uninvented, but they can be brought under reasonable control. The United States takes extraordinary precautions to assure that its nuclear weapons can never be used without the express authority of the president. This is one reason why the competence and character of candidates are such important issues at election time and why the president is often referred to as the "man with his finger on the button."

Beyond the normal precautions that governments take to protect their nuclear weapons (some countries thought to have nuclear weapons will not even admit their existence), countries will sometimes work together to limit the number of weapons or troops they maintain. This process is called arms control, and it is commonly considered the best hope, short of total disarmament, for reducing tension among nations.

The history of arms control has been a history of incremental advances in mutual security laced with decisive setbacks because of cheating or miscalculation. For example, in 1922 the United States, Great Britain, France, Italy, and Japan signed an arms control treaty in which they promised to limit the number of battleships they would retain. But because the agreement pertained only to large ships, the Japanese began building many smaller ships, which they used to promote their aggressive military policies in the 1930s and during World War II. Arms control treaties signed by the United States and the Soviet Union in the 1960s, on the other hand, have held up and have made the world a slightly more stable place.

In 1987, President Reagan signed an arms control treaty with Soviet leader Mikhail Gorbachev that would reduce for the first time the number of intermediate-range nuclear missiles that the two countries possess. Under President George Bush, the United States and the Soviet Union moved a step further toward disarmament. In early 1989, Mikhail Gorbachev promised drastic, unprecedented cuts in Soviet military expenditures, weaponry, and manpower, including the removal of 500,000 troops and 10,000 tanks from active duty. The two sides also have opened a dialogue about eliminating short-range missiles from Europe.

President Ronald Reagan and Soviet leader Mikhail Gorbachev sign the Intermediate-range Nuclear Forces (INF) Treaty in December 1987. Arms control treaties such as this one, in which the two nations promised to reduce the number of intermediate-range missiles they possess, are commonly considered the best hope, short of total disarmament, for reducing tension among nations.

In 1972, members of the Army National Guard clear debris from a bridge abutment after a dam break flooded an area of West Virginia. In addition to supplementing the regular armed forces in times of war, the National Guard is frequently mobilized in times of peace to help during emergencies such as natural disasters and riots.

The Military in Peacetime

Wars, especially large multinational wars such as World War I and World War II, are catastrophic events that forever change the world and the way people live. But the military's effect on society does not end when peace comes. Although the U.S. military establishment is deliberately kept at arm's length from the workings of the civil government, the American defense organization is so large and multifaceted that it cannot help but be an integral part of daily life in the United States.

One facet of the military that often contributes to the well-being of the United States in peacetime is the National Guard. The National Guard is the official militia of the United States—that is, it is America's nonprofessional citizen army consisting of more than 500,000 men and women who volunteer to be part-time soldiers, usually on weekends or on 2-week breaks from their

101

In 1988, Marine Junior Reserve Officer Training Corps (JROTC) cadets go through rifle movements during a drill competition at Lincoln High School in Yonkers, New York. ROTC cadets supplement each military service's staff of college-educated officers and attend courses in military theory, history, and leadership.

usual occupations. Most states have their own Army National Guard, and some also have an Air National Guard. These units normally come under the command of the state governor, but during a national emergency (such as the sudden outbreak of the Korean War in 1950), the National Guard can be placed under the authority of the president, as commander in chief, and integrated into the regular military.

Similarly, the army, air force, marines, and navy all have part-time reserve units that serve in a corresponding capacity. Both the National Guard and the Organized Reserves for the most part train with hand-me-down tanks, planes, and other equipment. The National Guard and the Organized Reserves make up about 30 percent of the nation's total military personnel. In contrast, active-duty military personnel make up 37 percent. Civilian support personnel constitute less than 20 percent, and retired military personnel constitute about 13 percent.

In addition to supplementing the regular armed forces in times of war, the National Guard and Organized Reserves are often called out for less extreme nonmilitary crises such as strikes, riots, and natural disasters. (In extreme situations, the regular military may be called into action as well.) For example, in 1970, the National Guard and regular army helped process and sort mail when U.S. postal workers went on strike.

The military also sponsors Reserve Officers' Training Corps (ROTC) programs at high schools and universities throughout America. Although each service conducts its own ROTC program, all are geared toward augmenting the military's staff of college-educated officers. Students enrolled in the ROTC attend classes in military theory and history and do course work designed to promote leadership and communication skills. Often the program includes some form of military training, such as flight training or naval experience at sea. In return for their commitment, ROTC members are eligible for academic scholarships and must serve a minimum of three years active duty or five years in the reserves upon graduation.

Another nonmilitary role of the nation's armed forces is in civil engineering. The system of interstate highways built in the 1950s and 1960s resulted from the Defense Department's belief that the country needed a nationwide road network for military purposes. Many of the Army Corps of Engineers' civil engineering projects—among them the Bonneville Dam on the Columbia River between Washington and Oregon, the Panama Canal, and Fort Peck Lake, a man-made lake in Montana—have benefited the civilian population more than they served any strict military purpose.

At a more subtle level, the Defense Department has influenced American life through its extensive activities in the areas of research and development. Research accounts for about 13 percent of the defense budget, not including the defense research conducted by the Department of Energy in such areas as nuclear weapons, the SDI, and reactors for the navy's nuclear submarines. The Pentagon is one of the largest investors in both basic and applied research in the areas of computer science, semiconductors, applied physics, metallurgy, telecommunications, medicine, chemistry, and advanced electronics. Economists have criticized the inefficiency of research and development projects slanted toward military purposes. But with American industry spending less for research and development, Pentagon research is among the best hopes for U.S. industry. Some of the areas in which the Pentagon is most interested include satellite imaging (a method of gaining detailed information about ground features through the use of satellite reconnaissance), hypersonic aircraft

Air Force officers at Mather Air Force Base in California participate in a program that will train them to become navigators. The DOD is especially interested in retaining highly skilled and experienced personnel because replacing them with new recruits can be more expensive in terms of hidden costs— technical training and decreased efficiency.

(planes that can fly in space and thus attain higher speeds), and high-definition television (televisions that produce images of greater clarity).

The Human Side of the Pentagon

It is a common misconception that the bulk of U.S. government spending goes to defense expenditures. The largest portion of government spending—about 60 percent—goes for governmental transfer payments to citizens in the form of welfare and Social Security. By comparison, the Pentagon receives about 27 percent of the total U.S. budget.

Similarly, the Pentagon's expenditures for high-priced hardware such as new bombers, missiles, and submarines receive the lion's share of attention at budget time—although the Defense Department spends nearly as much money meeting the human needs of its many dependents. About one-fourth of its budget goes for expenditures such as salaries, health care, training and education, housing, dependent child care, and retirement pensions.

Whether or not there is any fighting to be done, the Pentagon has many mouths to feed, many feet that need boots, and many heads to shelter. Because the DOD is responsible for the well-being of so many people—more than 3.2 million military and civilian employees and their families, as well as retired employees—policymakers and budget planners pay much attention to these human needs.

The Defense Department's demand for military personnel is essentially a budget problem: how much money to allocate for pay increases to attract new recruits. Similarly, the retention of experienced military personnel requires increased pay or bonuses in order to encourage these people to stay in the service. (Currently, military pay levels run about 11 percent less than competitive civilian pay for similar work.) The effort to retain experienced personnel is important because replacing them with new people can be much more expensive in terms of hidden costs, for example, technical and specialized training and decreased efficiency.

Since the end of the draft in the early 1970s, determining how much to spend for what level of manpower has been a fundamental question for Pentagon decision makers. In the Reagan era, the percentage of the total defense budget that went to military pay stayed roughly constant, whereas investment in new weapons systems shot up and then declined again. But over the years of the Reagan administration, pay increases helped bolster the average length of service, which rose from 5.55 years in 1981 to 6.25 years in 1988.

Military personnel are eligible for a pension after only 20 years of service; this means some people in the service retire before they reach the age of 40. In the private sector, the usual retirement age is 65, or even 70. Thus, a military pension costs the Defense Department as much as double or triple what a private-sector pension can, because military retirements last so much longer. In fiscal year 1989, the Pentagon paid out in retirement pay alone about $24 billion—an amount equal to the entire defense budget of Great Britain. These pension expenditures are a growing part of the Pentagon's financial burden and have increased to more than 10 percent of total budgetary spending. Many critics have insisted that this is an expense that must be brought under control, just as defense spending as a whole is going to have to be brought under control.

President-elect George Bush, President Ronald Reagan, and Soviet general secretary Mikhail Gorbachev take a break for sightseeing during the Soviet leader's visit to New York in December 1988. Recent advances between the two superpowers in the reduction of nuclear arms have contributed to a thawing of the Cold War.

SEVEN

The Challenge of National Security

From its inception—and increasingly so as the years have gone by—the DOD has been charged with vitally important political duties. More than a century before there was a Defense Department, Carl von Clausewitz (1780–1831), a Prussian military officer, wrote *On War*, a book about military strategy and the use of force by nations. In it, he wrote the now well known line "War is merely the continuation of political relations by other means." By this, he meant simply that nations use military force—or, more effectively, the threat of force—as a means to achieve their political goals when diplomacy, persuasion, or negotiation fail. In the case of the Pentagon, this concept has been used as a tool of American foreign policy—a policy charged with such gigantic responsibilities as maintaining the balance of power between the West and the Soviet bloc, of occupying Europe and much of Asia (not just Germany and Japan) in the aftermath of World War II, and of containing communism on both continents.

The United States has no empire like the empires maintained by Britain and France in the 17th, 18th, and 19th centuries, whereby these countries imposed their culture and political and economic system on colonies overseas. Since World War II, however, America has been the unofficial leader of the First World empire, the loose alliance of all the Western industrialized democracies. The United States has held this position of leadership not only because of its political and military strength but also because of its moral strength. But sometimes the reckless exercise of its political and military strength abroad has had the effect of eroding its moral authority. Such was the case in Iran in 1979, when the dictatorial shah of Iran (a U.S. ally who allowed Iran to be used for U.S. military purposes but who was also engaged in corruption and human-rights violations) was toppled by his own people.

Since World War II, the United States has expended the majority of its defense resources in preparation for a conflict with one or more members of the Communist bloc. But the conflicts of the postwar world in which the United States has actually been engaged were outside its World War II theaters of operation: Greece, Turkey, Korea, Guatemala, Nicaragua, Lebanon, Cuba, Vietnam, the Dominican Republic, Libya, and Grenada. In most of these cases (Korea and Vietnam excepted), U.S. involvement was either in the form of an extremely limited deployment of American forces or covert support of insurgents.

Controlling a Bureaucratic Giant

What began as the administrative union of the Department of War and the Department of the Navy has turned into an immense defense and national-security apparatus that has taken on a life of its own. There have been questions about whether or not the U.S. defense establishment is too big, too extensive, and too involved in the private sector to carry out its security mission unencumbered by extraneous factors, such as which congressman's district makes bolts or which defense contractor maintains the best hunting lodge for Pentagon decision makers.

Any examination of the Pentagon's conduct of national security inevitably points to bureaucratic habits that are actually detrimental to the search for security. For example, the Defense Department's quest for the highest-quality, best-designed, state-of-the-art equipment—a practice known as gold plating—leads to well-publicized abuses, such as $400 coffeepots and $600 toilet seats, as well as pricier mistakes. The Stealth bomber, for example, which by mid-1989 had cost the taxpayers $22 billion in development fees, may be cut altogether if some members of Congress have their way. The manner in which the Pentagon makes its business decisions is a steady source of grist for the congressional investigation mill, especially when there are so many revolving-door job exchanges between retiring Pentagon personnel leaving to work for defense contractors and defense executives entering government

In 1983, U.S. Marines walk down a street in Greenville, Grenada. After the prime minister of Grenada had been murdered by the Grenadian military in a violent overthrow of the Socialist government, leaders of neighboring nations asked the United States to assist in restoring order to the island.

American members of NATO's forces in West Germany drive down a street in Stockhausen during NATO's annual military exercises in 1983. Improved ties between Eastern and Western Europe in the late 1980s have raised serious questions about whether such displays of military strength will continue.

service. These exchanges appear to many as favoritism, bribery, and trafficking of confidential government documents (for instance, specifications for proposed weapons).

Another well-known flaw of the Pentagon's bureaucratic practice is inertia in its actions and strategy. Many people ask why the United States must continue to pay for the defense of once-ravaged Japan and Europe now that they are healthy industrial economies themselves. Others wonder how the Pentagon, being so large and multifaceted, can possibly keep pace with the need for ever-greater levels of secrecy. Secrecy is important to national security, but in the 1980s it was taken so far that staff members of the NSC essentially planned and financed a private war against Nicaragua from the White House basement, presumably without the president's knowledge or congressional approval.

Toward Pentagon Reform

During the transition from the Reagan administration to the Bush administration, there was much discussion about reforming traditional notions of Defense Department procurement practices. Policymakers questioned the necessity of matching or exceeding potential adversaries weapon for weapon, soldier for soldier. In the Reagan-Weinberger years, one formula ruled procurement decisions: *More* is better. With tighter budgets in the Bush era, more attention has been focused on how to do more with less. The name for this common-sense notion is competitive strategies, or trying to exploit a potential enemy's weaknesses by playing on one's own strengths (for instance, advanced technology) for the lowest possible price.

Furthermore, there are serious questions as to whether the border between Eastern and Western Europe (better known as the iron curtain) will continue to be the focus of East-West tensions or whether East-West tensions will continue to have the same meaning in the future that they have had in the past. Whatever the answers may be, the DOD will have to wrestle with the challenges and contradictions of its mission to preserve America's national security. These challenges will, no doubt, continue to shape the structure and focus of the DOD.

Department of Defense

SECRETARY OF DEFENSE
DEPUTY SECRETARY OF DEFENSE

DEPARTMENT OF THE ARMY

SECRETARY OF THE ARMY

UNDER SECRETARY AND ASSISTANT SECRETARIES OF THE ARMY	CHIEF OF STAFF, ARMY

ARMY MAJOR COMMANDS AND AGENCIES

DEPARTMENT OF THE AIR FORCE

SECRETARY OF THE AIR FORCE

UNDER SECRETARY AND ASSISTANT SECRETARIES OF THE AIR FORCE	CHIEF OF STAFF, AIR FORCE

AIR FORCE MAJOR COMMANDS AND AGENCIES

INSPECTOR GENERAL

GENERAL COUNSEL

DEPARTMENT OF THE NAVY

SECRETARY OF THE NAVY

UNDER SECRETARY AND ASSISTANT SECRETARIES OF THE NAVY	CHIEF OF NAVAL OPERATIONS	COMMANDANT OF THE MARINE CORPS

NAVY MAJOR COMMANDS AND AGENCIES

MARINE CORPS MAJOR COMMANDS AND AGENCIES

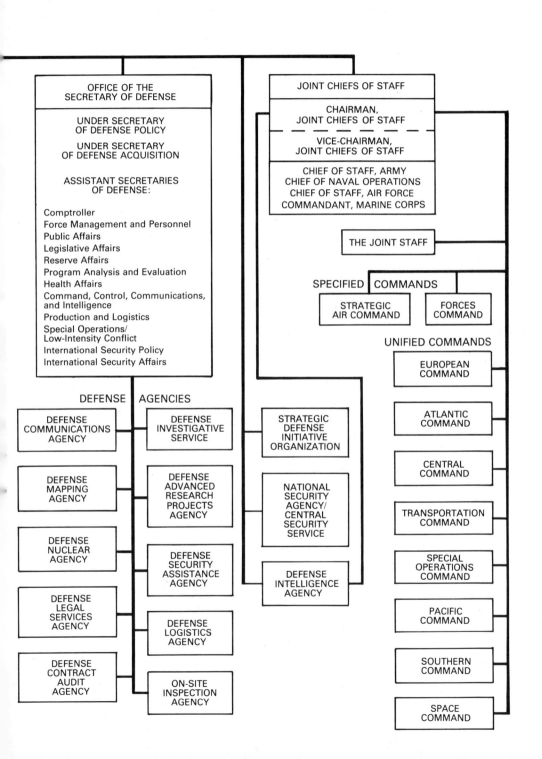

OFFICE OF THE
SECRETARY OF DEFENSE

UNDER SECRETARY
OF DEFENSE POLICY

UNDER SECRETARY
OF DEFENSE ACQUISITION

ASSISTANT SECRETARIES
OF DEFENSE:

Comptroller
Force Management and Personnel
Public Affairs
Legislative Affairs
Reserve Affairs
Program Analysis and Evaluation
Health Affairs
Command, Control, Communications,
and Intelligence
Production and Logistics
Special Operations/
Low-Intensity Conflict
International Security Policy
International Security Affairs

JOINT CHIEFS OF STAFF

CHAIRMAN,
JOINT CHIEFS OF STAFF

VICE-CHAIRMAN,
JOINT CHIEFS OF STAFF

CHIEF OF STAFF, ARMY
CHIEF OF NAVAL OPERATIONS
CHIEF OF STAFF, AIR FORCE
COMMANDANT, MARINE CORPS

THE JOINT STAFF

SPECIFIED COMMANDS

STRATEGIC
AIR COMMAND

FORCES
COMMAND

UNIFIED COMMANDS

EUROPEAN
COMMAND

ATLANTIC
COMMAND

CENTRAL
COMMAND

TRANSPORTATION
COMMAND

SPECIAL
OPERATIONS
COMMAND

PACIFIC
COMMAND

SOUTHERN
COMMAND

SPACE
COMMAND

DEFENSE AGENCIES

DEFENSE
COMMUNICATIONS
AGENCY

DEFENSE
INVESTIGATIVE
SERVICE

STRATEGIC
DEFENSE
INITIATIVE
ORGANIZATION

DEFENSE
MAPPING
AGENCY

DEFENSE
ADVANCED
RESEARCH
PROJECTS
AGENCY

NATIONAL
SECURITY
AGENCY/
CENTRAL
SECURITY
SERVICE

DEFENSE
NUCLEAR
AGENCY

DEFENSE
SECURITY
ASSISTANCE
AGENCY

DEFENSE
INTELLIGENCE
AGENCY

DEFENSE
LEGAL
SERVICES
AGENCY

DEFENSE
LOGISTICS
AGENCY

DEFENSE
CONTRACT
AUDIT
AGENCY

ON-SITE
INSPECTION
AGENCY

GLOSSARY

Cold War   A conflict over ideological differences (such as that between the United States and the Soviet Union) conducted not with arms but with power politics, economic pressure, espionage, and hostile propaganda.

Containment   The policy, process, or result of preventing the expansion of a hostile ideology or power.

Deterrence   The idea that the United States and its allies can prevent, or deter, a nuclear attack by vowing to launch a retaliatory nuclear attack if fired upon.

Joint Chiefs of Staff (JCS)   An advisory group made up of the military heads of each service that assists the president and secretary of defense in the direction and planning of the armed forces. The JCS is composed of the chief of staff of the army, the chief of staff of the air force, the chief of naval operations, the commandant of the Marine Corps, a chairman, and a vice-chairman.

Militia   A civilian defense force made up of citizen-soldiers.

National Security Council (NSC)   A seven-member council that advises the president on the coordination of domestic, foreign, and military policies relating to national security. Among the members of the NSC is the secretary of defense.

North Atlantic Treaty Organization (NATO)   An organization formed by the United States and its allies in 1949 to counter the military buildup of Communist forces in Eastern Europe. The members of NATO have pledged to defend each other if any one of them is attacked by a hostile nation.

Specified Command   Forces headed by a single service branch but which serve the needs of the entire defense establishment; for example, the Strategic Air Command.

Unified Command   Forces made up of two or more of the armed services that work together under a single commander; for example, the Space Command.

SELECTED REFERENCES

Ambrose, Stephen E., and James A. Barber, Jr., eds. *The Military and American Society.* New York: Free Press, 1972.

Boffey, Philip M. et al. *Claiming the Heavens: The New York Times Complete Guide to the Star Wars Debate.* New York: Times Books, 1988.

Department of Defense. *Annual Report to the Congress (FY 1988–89).* Washington, DC: U.S. Government Printing Office, 1988.

Dunnigan, James F. *How to Make War: All the World's Weapons, Armed Forces and Tactics.* New York: Morrow, 1982.

Fallows, James. *National Defense.* New York: Random House, 1981.

Kaplan, Fred. *The Wizards of Armageddon.* New York: Simon & Schuster, 1983.

Kinnard, Douglas. *The Secretary of Defense.* Lexington: University Press of Kentucky, 1980.

Luttwak, Edward N. *The Pentagon and the Art of War.* New York: Simon & Schuster, 1985.

Perry, Mark. *Four Stars: The Inside Story of the Forty-Year Battle Between the Joint Chiefs of Staff and America's Civilian Leaders.* Boston: Houghton Mifflin, 1989.

Rasor, Dina. *The Pentagon Underground.* New York: Times Books, 1985.

Ries, John C. *The Management of Defense.* Baltimore: Johns Hopkins University Press, 1964.

Rovner, Mark. *Defense Dollars and Sense: A Common Cause Guide to the Defense Budget Process.* Washington, DC: Common Cause, 1983.

Stubbing, Richard A., and Richard A. Mendel. *The Defense Game: An Insider Explores the Astonishing Realities of America's Defense Establishment.* New York: Harper & Row, 1986.

Tobias, Sheila et al. *What Kinds of Guns Are They Buying for Your Butter?: A Beginner's Guide to Defense, Weaponry, and Military Spending.* New York: Morrow, 1982.

Trask, Roger R. *The Secretaries of Defense: A Brief History 1947–85.* Washington, DC: Historical Office, Office of the Secretary of Defense, 1985.

INDEX

118

Andrew Cohen works in the New York news bureau of *The Wall Street Journal*. He holds a B.A. from Columbia University, where he studied history and political science.

Beth Heinsohn is an editor and reporter for Platt's Global Alert, a petroleum industry newswire. She holds an A.B. from Bryn Mawr College and an M.I.A. from the Columbia University School of International and Public Affairs.

Arthur M. Schlesinger, jr., served in the White House as special assistant to Presidents Kennedy and Johnson. He is the author of numerous acclaimed works in American history and has twice been awarded the Pulitzer Prize. He taught history at Harvard College for many years and is currently Albert Schweitzer Professor of the Humanities at the City College of New York.